DETAINED IN ENGLAND
1914-1920
EASTCOTE POW CAMP
PATTISHALL

A brief, illustrated history

Colin R Chapman & *S Richard Moss*

Colin Chapman has pursued local, social and family history since the age of seven and discovered that almost all of his ancestors originate from Northamptonshire and adjacent counties. He has written fourteen genealogically-related books and he lectures on allied topics throughout the English-speaking world. He is President of the Northamptonshire Family History Society and a Fellow of the Society of Genealogists. He originated the alpha-three code to identify British Isles counties that formed the basis of British and international standards. He is Lord of the Manor of Pattishall.

Richard Moss has spent a life-time in teaching history to young and old in traditional grammar, primary and secondary schools, teacher-training colleges, universities, local history groups and in various locations including: village halls, parish churches, cathedrals, country houses, fields and hearth-sides in Liverpool, St Helens, Kirby, Pattishall, Towcester and Northampton. He has a lifelong interest in local history in particular Pattishall where his interest in Eastcote Camp was aroused. In 2010 he moved to Staffordshire where he has continued his enthusiasm with the past.

Published by
LOCHIN PUBLISHING
19 Woodmancote, Dursley, GL11 4AF, England

First Edition 2012 (978 1 873686 22 5)

Copyright of the Authors and Lochin Publishing Society 2012

> British Library Cataloguing in Publication Data
> Chapman, Colin R, 1939-
> Moss, S Richard, 1933-
> Detained in England 1914-1920: Eastcote POW Camp, Pattishall
>
> A catalogue record for this book
> is available from the British Library
>
> ISBN 978 1 873686 22 5

CONTENTS

List of Illustrations	p.v
Preface	p.vii
Chapter 1. Why Eastcote?	p.1
Chapter 2. The Camp: Phase I, 1914-1915	p.12
Chapter 3. The Camp: Phase II, 1915-1919	p.18
Chapter 4. Escapees	p.32
Chapter 5. Prisoners' Lives and Letters	p.37
Chapter 6. The Camp: Phase III, post-1919	p.52
Chapter 7. Epilogue	p.58
Bibliography and References	p.59
Index of Names	p.60
Index of Places	p.63

[*Milton Keynes did not exist in 1914-1920 and is included here for interest only*]

Geographical Location of Pattishall

LIST OF ILLUSTRATIONS

Fronticepiece. Geographical location of Pattishall (A Miles)

Fig 1.1. Eastcote House, Pattishall (J Lees postcard)

Fig 1.2. 1911 Census return of Eastcote House (The National Archives)

Fig 1.3. Internees at Olympia, 1914 (Illustrated War News)

Fig 1.4. Alton Abbey, Hampshire 2012 (C Chapman)

Fig 1.5. Rev George Gibson, Vicar of Pattishall 1897-1924 (R Moss)

Fig 1.6. Boy Scouts guarding Eastcote House, 1914 (Northampton Independent)

Fig 1.7. Men marching to Frith Hill Camp, Surrey (C Chapman)

Fig 1.8. Sale of land by Malsbury to Hopkins and McGhee (R Hawtin)

Fig 1.9. Location of Eastcote House in Pattishall (R Hawtin)

Fig 2.1. Model harbour with POWs (J Lees postcard)

Fig 2.2. POWs tending gardens (ICRC postcard)

Fig 2.3. Model harbour with sailing boats (J Lees postcard)

Fig 2.4. *RMS Lusitania* commemorative medal (C Chapman)

Fig 2.5. Interior of camp theatre (1916 book)

Fig 2.6. Map of railway networks, c.1911 (C Chapman)

Fig 3.1. Some of the Eastcote POWs (1916 book)

Fig 3.2. POWs in dormitory hut (1916 book)

Fig 3.3. POW bakers at work (1916 book)

Fig 3.4. Guard and bored POWs (1916 book)

Fig 3.5. 'Official' Camp Christmas Card 1916

Fig 3.6. POWs and watch tower (1916 book)

Fig 3.7. POW Krauplatz at Pattishall (C Chapman)

Fig 3.8. Camp theatre performance (C Chapman)

Fig 3.9. Pattishall Camp guards (I Illingworth)

Fig 4.1. Eastcote Camp, general view (1916 book)
Fig 4.2. POW Horner, repatriated to Germany (A Nightingale)
Fig 4.3. Reverse of Fig 4.2. (from Horner to William Nightingale)
Fig 4.4. The *Bertha* (J Coy & G Perrett)

Fig 5.1. POW Clauberg's letter (C Chapman)
Fig 5.2. Inkpot from Pattishall Camp (R Moss)
Fig 5.3. POW Schmidt and fellow POWs at Pattishall (G Schmidt)
Fig 5.4. POW Schmidt and fellow POWs at Descote Quarry (G Schmidt)
Fig 5.5. POW Wiedemann's service book and identity disc (C Chapman)
Fig 5.6. POW Salbenblatt's identity disc (A Nightingale)
Fig 5.7. POW Albrecht's 102nd letter (C Chapman)
Fig 5.8. Musketier Krental wearing Iron Cross (W Palang)
Fig 5.9. The *Orotava* (W Palang)
Fig 5.10. POW Krental at Mendlesham (W Palang)

Fig 6.1. Camp Guards' Quarters, later Pattishall Village Hall (I Illingworth)
Fig 6.2. POW Graves in Pattishall Churchyard Extension (I Illingworth)
Fig 6.3. Pattishall POW Graves at Cannock Chase (C Chapman)

Book cover. Pattishall POWs (1916 book) & Pattishall Schoolchildren (M Waller)

The 1916 book referred to above was published in a variety of sizes and formats in both English and German, the English title being *German Prisoners in Great Britain*. No publisher is stated on the English editions and there is no explanatory text; it was printed by Tillotson & Son Ltd of Bolton and London. German editions (*Deutsche Kriegsgefangene in Gross-Britannien*) include several pages of accompanying text. The photographs were taken by members of the photographic section of the Royal Flying Corps at the request of the American Ambassador in Berlin to form part of the Wurtemberg War Exhibition.

PREFACE

It is likely that many of today's inhabitants of Pattishall in Northamptonshire are unaware that almost 100 years ago there were well over four thousand men living in the parish behind a barbed wire enclosure with tall lookout towers, arc lights, and armed guards parading its perimeter. Now, every time when they travel eastwards along Banbury Lane, turn right into Pound Lane and thence turn down Bird's Hill Road, and turn right again at the junction facing the school to re-join Banbury Lane, they are tracing the boundary of a First World War Prisoner of War Camp, known initially as Eastcote, and later, Pattishall Camp.

This booklet tells the story of that Camp, how it came into existence during The Great War of 1914-19 and the daily lives of those Germans, Austrians and others incarcerated therein. It is a tale drawn from the memories of contemporary parishioners, from public and Trade Union archives, reports of official inspections of the Camp, personal letters, maps, photographs, artefacts, buildings and topography. We trust that in putting this record into print we are offering the community another piece of the jig-saw of Pattishall's little-known but remarkable history.

There are many to whom thanks are due who have provided us with valuable material, ideas and a great deal more: Robert and Jennifer Hawtin of Bay Farm Eastcote, on whose land much of the Camp stood, for their enthusiasm and material help; Pat and David Rowden of Eastcote House, for information and photographs; Austin Nightingale for the loan of his papers about the Camp and the work of the late Dr Frank Foden; John Coy, for permission to photograph 'Bertha' the model ship; Marion Waller, for her photographs and memories; Wolfgang Paland and Günter Schmidt for letters written by their grandfathers whilst POWs in the Camp; Graham Mark, Derek Smeathers and Neville Watterson, for the loan of other prisoners' letters and their translation; Otto Raffelstetter and James Brannan for deciphering and translating yet other letters written in the old German script by POWs held in the Camp and its satellites; Rev Robert Miller for detail on Father Hopkins; David Wilcock for drawing our attention to the report in a Suffolk newspaper on three escapees; Aled Jones for directing us to documents in the Library of Congress; Iris Illingworth and the Pattishall History Group, for patiently allowing us to talk to them and by doing so clarify our thoughts. The librarians, archivists and keepers of collections in Northamptonshire, the University of Warwick, the Principal Probate Registry, The British Library - Newspapers, The National Archives, the Imperial War Museum, the Commonwealth War Graves Commission, the Volksbund Deutsche Kriegsgräberfürsorge in Germany and the Library of Congress in the United States have been both helpful and courteous in making source materials available to us. To Margaret Moss we owe especial thanks for providing warm hospitality and harmony during our work together. The contributions of Emily Moss in designing the cover and of Adam Miles in preparing the location map of Pattishall are particularly appreciated. For any others whom we have omitted to acknowledge here, we offer our apologies yet gratitude.

This booklet began by both of us working in 'isolation', confined in our separate 'camps' and it was Graham Mark who, unknowingly but fortuitously, put us back in touch with each other. His book *Prisoners of War in British Hands during WWI* provided the catalyst for us to pursue our investigations and progress this work.

A fuller account of 'our' camp, particularly of its background and its one hundred and sixty or more satellite working camps scattered across south-eastern England, East Anglia and the Home Counties during The Great War, may be found in Chapman's *Pattishall, Enemy Aliens & 160 Dependent POW Camps, 1914-20* – see Bibliography.

* * * * *

Until 1971 monetary values in Britain were expressed in pounds, shillings and pence (£.s.d.) with a pound comprising twenty shillings and a shilling comprising twelve pennies – equivalent to today's 5p. A penny comprised two half-pennies, pronounced *haypennies*. A quarter of a penny was termed a farthing. In writing monetary values, two styles were commonly used during the Great War. For example, ten shillings and sixpence could be expressed as 10s. 6d. or as 10/6; seven-pence and three farthings would appear as 7¾d. In the following pages we have repeated the styles as used by different individuals in their own reports and letters.

* * * * *

We should point out that the land on which the Eastcote/Pattishall Camp stood is now privately owned and is not freely open to public access. Persons wishing to explore the site should seek permission from the current owner.

1. WHY EASTCOTE?

One might well ask why put a detention centre for aliens and foreign nationals in the middle of a quiet corner of Northamptonshire. Well, its location in Pattishall parish is geographically pretty central; indeed only five miles from Weedon, a military focal point for George III at the time of the Napoleonic Wars, and close to the Grand Junction Canal, the Watling Street (now the A5) and, by 1914, the railways. Such considerations came after the event rather than in determining it.

If we are looking further for an answer we could start with a house – Eastcote House (Fig.1.1) on the corner at the top of Bird's Hill Road at its junction with Pound Lane. The house, its history and the families who lived in it have been thoroughly examined by us over many years. As a result we have discovered that by 1914 several people who, not entirely by chance, were drawn together in the story. Firstly there were the owners of the house, Constance Gresham (widow of the late Francis Wiseman) and her husband Frederick Gresham; secondly, three men, Charles Plomer Hopkins, Joseph Havelock Wilson and Richard McGhee, drawn together by a common concern – provision of accommodation for certain merchant seamen made destitute by the outbreak of war.

But let us go back to 1796 when Thomas Pirkins, the Lord of both of Pattishall's manors since 1791, and his wife Sarah, completed the rebuilding of this manor house. (The other manor house in Pattishall also remains standing today as Manor Farm beside the Holy Cross parish church, and the two manors themselves had effectively already been amalgamated, but such facts need not concern us here.) Thomas and Sarah Pirkins marked their achievement by having **T/S/P 1796** cast onto the lead rainwater hoppers surviving nowadays at both ends of the slate roof. The water supply to the house warrants some attention for its ingenuity: a hydraulic ram in a pit situated in fields formerly called 'Home Ground' pumped water up to Eastcote House and its outbuildings. The pump, to which we shall refer again later, remained in use until the late 1950s. In addition to the main house, Thomas and Sarah owned a coach house on its south side, a stable block and a large barn with threshing space between two tall opposable doors: evidently a working farm as well as incorporating a grand dwelling, although it is identified modestly in most 19th century records simply as a "farm house".

It was only after 1871 that the name Eastcote House came to be used, while Philip Grove – "a tiller of the soil" as he was termed in an earlier census - and his family were occupying the farm. By 1891 Matthew Wise Phipps (62), from Emberton, Buckinghamshire and his wife Sarah (64), a daughter of Thomas and Mary Gleed Howes of Northampton, had moved into Eastcote House. Phipps described himself as "living on private means". This branch of the Phipps family originated in Abington, Cambridgeshire, contrary to local legend.

An indenture of March 1897 confirmed the sale of Eastcote House by Matthew Phipps to the widower John Francis Wiseman. Wiseman had been born in 1851 in Glasgow, the son of East India merchant, James Wiseman and his wife, Lydia. Although John Wiseman's name appears clearly on the documentation of 25th March, his mother later claimed (in a Chancery Court case in 1908) that it was she who had bought the house and she lived there with him. Whatever the true situation, Francis Wiseman, as he was better known, took up residence in Eastcote House during 1897. A year later he remarried, this time to Constance Ida Halcombe of Putney, eight years his junior. His parents had long lives: Francis's father James died in 1903 at 83 leaving an estate of nearly £118,840 and his mother Lydia in 1912 aged 90. Francis was not so long lived and Constance Wiseman was widowed in May 1907.

Forty-seven year-old Constance Wiseman did not remain a widow for very long. In the summer of 1910, she caught the eye of Frederick Gresham a 71 year-old journalist, born in Bedfordshire, formerly in the tanning and currier business, and they married. Frederick's regard for dogs is evidenced by the kennelman at their home (Fig.1.2). It is clear that at this time Constance held the major interest in the house. Frederick and his younger wife were residing at Eastcote in the late summer of 1914 when their world was changed forever.

At midnight on 4th/5th August 1914, war erupted between Britain and Germany. There were many foreign nationals, seamen, businessmen, professionals, and married men and women of Germanic origin living in Britain and in British colonies overseas. Considerable numbers of persons with German-sounding names had resided peacefully on British soils for more than a generation. What to do with men and women, some officially classified as aliens, and merely because they happened to reside in a territory at war with their own, had long been an international problem. Some posed a potential risk, if acting as spies or saboteurs, while others happily became loyal to their adopted countries of residence. It had been customary, worldwide, to round up and intern all 'foreigners' in times of war, just in case they might act disloyally, and to term them 'Prisoners of War'. As the interned were concentrated in particular locations such places were termed Concentration Camps, although this description later took on a deeply sinister and emotional connotation.

British handling of POWs had received a mixed press. In 1902, during the Boer War, old men and boys from the eastern Transvaal taken in the previous December were shipped to Madras, the port for The Wellington Parolers's Camp 6,000 feet up in the Nilgiri Hills. Another contingent was sent to Broad Bottom Camp on the Island of St Helena. Sadly these centres, like those on the South African veldt, were scenes of great deprivation and hardship. But Britain was not alone in harshly treating some of its POWs and, as a consequence, in 1906 and 1907 international meetings were convened in Switzerland and Holland to agree on parameters for the future handling and treatment of wounded combatants and prisoners of war. Thus the 1906 Geneva Convention and the 1907 Hague Convention offered guidance to warring nations on how to deal with civilian internees and military, combatant, prisoners. These agreements, however, were based primarily on experiences of the Boer War and earlier conflicts, which involved minimal numbers of wounded and captured persons compared with those encountered as The Great War developed; varying interpretations and applications of the agreements by Germany and Britain and their allies from 1914 led to many arguments and then reprisals by the governments of both sides. The neutral powers, initially the United States of America and then from 1917, Sweden and Switzerland, through their embassies, had their work cut out acting as intermediaries, forwarding correspondence from government officials and prisoners themselves, visiting POW Camps as 'neutral' inspectors, and settling many inter-governmental disputes.

Dealing with aliens in Britain at the outbreak of The Great War was the responsibility of the Home Office. However, both the War Office and the Foreign Office quickly established POW Departments although that of the War Office was attached to the Home Office, and the Admiralty also set up a POW Department. The lack of clear identification of responsibility led to some inter-departmental rivalry and multiplication of effort, as is apparent from the correspondence and related documentation now held in The National Archives. On 5th August 1914 the Aliens' Restriction Act defined aliens as either 'friendly' or 'unfriendly'. But the British Government was in part influenced by public opinion and also by the course of events the war took. Rumours of German atrocities on Belgian women and children rapidly created a wave of anti-German hysteria in Britain. On 8th August the Defence of the

Realm Act (DORA) facilitated the rounding up of male German nationals of military age; many were sent hastily to Olympia (Fig.1.3), Horsham, York and Dublin. It was a pressing problem, and even by the end of 1914, when many of those initially interned had been interviewed and released, the POW population in Britain stood at 17,433 civilians and 6,388 military (including naval) personnel. A major problem, besides the vast numbers involved, was that civilian internees, unlike combatants, were generally unaccustomed to discipline imposed by the rigours of war; thus confinement, often with little or nothing to do, led to frustration, boredom and mental disorientation.

In Britain there were those who, long before the war and especially at the outbreak of hostilities, were deeply committed to the interests of merchant seamen and their families of all nationalities. It was at this moment that the world of Frederick and Constance Gresham at Eastcote House was over-turned. Into their lives came three men with other priorities. The first of these, Charles Plomer Hopkins, was possibly known to them. The other two, Joseph Havelock Wilson and Richard McGhee, would not have come quickly to their minds unless in perusing national newspapers their interest had been drawn to the activities during the previous decade of merchant seamen, dock-workers and Trade Unionists.

Born in 1861, Charles Plomer Hopkins had a long and active life assisting ordinary seamen, in which capacity he came into contact with the National Sailors' and Firemen's Union (NSFU). He had lived and worked in India and Burma. In Rangoon, where he had trained for the priesthood, and ordained in 1885 by its Anglican bishop (though never licensed to practise in England), and in also Calcutta, he set up small mission centres for seamen. It may have been in this work that he met James Wiseman the East India merchant. As we have seen, James's son, Francis Wiseman, was Constance Gresham's first husband. Francis Wiseman had lived in Pattishall from 1897 so it is possible that through this link Hopkins became aware of Eastcote House and its potential as a home for needy merchant seamen. Hopkins had previously obtained a property at Barry Dock that he utilised as a Seamen's Refuge or Mission, but finding this too restricted for his aspirations he acquired premises in south-east London which became known as Greenwich Priory; this also provided a useful London base for his various activities in the Capital. Needing a more tranquil environment for the religious side of his work, he subsequently purchased land in Beech near Alton in Hampshire to establish another centre, based on Benedictine principles. As head of the order he was known as Father Michael Hopkins. With help from men drawn into the order, in 1901 Hopkins began the construction of a small Abbey there. In 1911 he was appointed Secretary to the International Committee of Seamen's Unions. In this capacity and related work he helped to settle the bitter seamen's strike of 1911-12 earning the respect of both unions and ship-owners, while also becoming a trustee of the NSFU.

Joseph Havelock Wilson was very different from Hopkins, although both shared a concern for the welfare of merchant seamen. Born in a Sunderland pub (the *General Havelock*) kept by his mother in 1858, Wilson ran off to sea as a young lad. Working in difficult conditions he saw the plight of his fellow workers and that his task was to ameliorate them. In 1887 he created the first seamen's union and in 1892 became Liberal MP for Middlesborough, but stood down in 1910 to focus on union work. The union he founded had collapsed in 1893 but he established the NSFU on sounder lines in 1894, becoming its General President. Experience taught him to value co-operation rather than confrontation, though this was to gain him a reputation amongst the rank and file as a 'bosses-man'. Together with an old friend and fellow Trade Unionist, Capt Edward (Ted) Tupper, he perceived far-left conspiracies at work in the heart of some unions. These were views he and Tupper apparently shared with Winston Churchill and certainly gained him the dislike of men like Emmanuel Shinwell. By 1914, yet badly crippled with rheumatism, Wilson was still General President of the NSFU, and deep passion for his Union and its members drove him on.

Richard McGhee, an Irish Protestant MP from 1896, was the third member of the trio. Born in 1851 McGhee became a committed Trade Unionist; he had been instrumental in founding the National Union of Dock Labourers in 1889 and was its first President. He had first met Wilson in Glasgow in 1887, then in Parliament, and later often worked with the seamen's unions; from 1914 until at least 1925 he also was a trustee of the NSFU. Although a Protestant, McGhee was a keen supporter of home rule for Ireland and, very much like Wilson, was anxious to achieve his aims through peaceful negotiation.

On 7th August 1914, with Father Hopkins in the Chair because of the illness of Wilson their usual Chairman, the Finance Committee of the NSFU resolved to: "instruct the Executive Officers...that should the need arise for the establishment of a concentration camp for the reception of...Alien Seamen, such a camp should be established." [Ref.1.1]. Alton Abbey was suggested for this purpose. By Alien Seamen the Committee meant the German merchant seamen members of the NSFU; Wilson had set up a German branch of his first union in 1889, long before there was open antagonism between Germany and Britain.

Four days later, true to his calling, Hopkins went directly to Stepney Police Court and offered Alton Abbey (Fig.1.4) as a detention centre for those alien merchant seamen currently attending the court. The clerk to the court, Albert Lieck, wrote in his own hand of the offer to the Under Secretary of State at the Home Office; the Home Secretary agreed immediately that those seamen whom the magistrate found without criminal intentions should be accommodated at Alton. Shortly afterwards the site was inspected by government officials and approval given for Hopkins to house a maximum of two hundred internees in the Abbey grounds on a temporary basis. Hopkins and two of the German seamen internees were among those later buried in the small cemetery at Alton Abbey (see Chapter 6).

While these arrangements were being put in place, the NSFU was aware that many more than 200 German merchant seamen were likely to be affected. Accordingly, an emergency meeting of its Finance Committee was convened on 31st August to take steps to obtain a suitable estate to establish a detention camp for alien seamen. With Wilson back in the Chair, it was agreed such a place should be used eventually to provide "….homes for worn-out members of the Union…". In parallel with these discussions, Hopkins again personally approached the government and now offered his Greenwich Priory as accommodation for further German merchant seamen. By 15th September this also was inspected and approval given to what was described in an internal memo within the Home Office as "a small and harmless specimen of the Alton Abbey home".

Things were moving swiftly, and at a meeting of the NSFU Executive Council on 19th September it was reported that in the search for suitable sites to establish camps for its German members "a contract had been entered into for the purchase of an estate at Eastcote, Pattishall, Northamptonshire" and that "a number of men were already at work getting the place ready for a large number of men". There seems to have been some imagination used here, for the formal conveyance of the property was not ratified until 9th November and then it was from Constance Gresham to McGhee and Hopkins; neither Wilson nor the NSFU are mentioned in the documentation. Mrs Gresham received £1,850 for Eastcote House, the stables, coach house, barn, cottages and land around the house. But to return to the meeting on 19th September, Wilson said that arrangements were in hand with the Government for funding at 10/- per man per week; these moves were endorsed by the Council which expressed "its hearty approval of the action taken by the President and the Finance Committee....".

On the same day J D Kellie MacCallum, Chief Constable of Northamptonshire, wrote to the Under Secretary of State at the Home Office describing the provision of a camp at Eastcote about to house 60 aliens, while assuring the Minister of the presence of a police guard (eventually of 14 men, some billetted on local residents) armed with cutlasses – a Gilbertian touch.

The British Government had a number of departments, agencies and organisations on which to call at this time. The Home Office initially looked after the civilian aliens. Within the War Office, a section of the Adjutant General's Department took responsibility for POWs, headed by Sir Herbert Belfield. That section became the Directorate of Prisoners of War in February 1915. In compliance with the 1907 Hague Convention, the POW Information Bureau (POWIB) was set up by mid-August 1914, to maintain a comprehensive database (on cards) and to respond to queries on all POWs, internees and combatants held by the British throughout the Empire. This was a War Office agency under the direction of Sir Paul Harvey whose staff, all speaking German, were civilians mostly drafted in from various branches of the civil service. Information on British POWs, civilian and combatant, was maintained by similar bureaux set up by Britain's enemies in their territories, also following the international Conventions. A Destitute Aliens Committee (DAC) under the chairmanship of Sir William Byrne was created on 20th August with three main aims: to organise the repatriation of certain classes of aliens - those not posing an immediate threat to Britain, to coordinate the efforts of a number of charities seeking to aid specific alien groups, and to make any special arrangements to accommodate and maintain destitute aliens referred from the Home Office, the War Office, and the Local Government Board. Its involvement with Eastcote is described below. The name of the DAC was changed to the Civilian Internment Camps Committee in November 1916, but by then Eastcote had ceased to house civilian aliens, as we shall see.

Various unofficial and largely uncoordinated welfare committees mushroomed across Britain to gather comforts such as clothing, food and tobacco to send to British POWs held in German camps. These groups were brought together within the War Office in September

1916 and managed by a committee Chaired by Sir Starr Jameson. Similar groups and individuals in Germany and Austria later sent parcels to their nationals held as POWs in British Camps, but two outstanding men in London also championed welfare committees specifically to benefit German POWs. The first, Dr K E Markel, a German chemist who had been living in England for over 30 years, had access to funds that he subsequently made available to provide books, musical instruments and tools at many POW camps in Britain. The second, Edward G Lowry, a senior attaché at the American Embassy in London, also had access to funds, some from the German Government, that he was authorised to spend on Germans held in Britain. Both Markel and Lowry Committees became well cherished by all of Britain's 'enemy aliens', including those held at Eastcote/Pattishall Camp.

The International Committee of the Red Cross (ICRC) had sent a circular from its Geneva headquarters to all the national Red Cross Societies on 15th August 1914, seeking support in caring for those beginning to suffer from the ravages of war. On 27th August it established the International Prisoners of War Agency to collate information on captured and wounded combatants, working with the warring nations but clearly maintaining a neutral stance throughout. The ICRC had no mandate for these activities, but the belligerent states greatly respected its work as it encouraged all sides to comply with the Geneva and Hague Conventions. The POWIB, for example, regularly sent copies of its data to the ICRC. The YMCA and the Quakers (Religious Society of Friends) also set up networks of local secretaries and visitors to counsel and provide practical help, particularly to civilian internees. The important involvement of these latter two organisations at Eastcote/Pattishall is described in Chapman's more comprehensive account of the Camp and its satellites (see Bibliography), although both receive passing mentions in the pages that follow.

At a meeting of Towcester Rural District Council (RDC) on 22nd September 1914 George E Groom, a Pattishall councillor, drew the attention of his colleagues to the Camp's existence and asked that the Medical Officer be sent to report on its state. There was a presumption locally that the Camp came directly under the control of the Crown, whereas in fact at the time it was in the names of NSFU trustees with the Home Office having responsibility for security. Whilst some residents were unhappy with the RDC's replies to their concerns they might have been even more worried to hear that in responding to an application by Wilson, the RDC gave him a licence to store 2½ tons of calcium carbide on the property – we presume as a source of acetylene for lighting. "The Inspector said the place proposed was satisfactory." [Ref.1.2].

On 22nd October Towcester RDC considered a letter from the Vicar of Pattishall, Rev George Gibson (Fig.1.5), in which "he had been informed the Sewage of the Camp from 1,500 to 2,000 men was being conducted into the brook." The RDC was told that the Home Office had sent Sir William Burr and Dr Bond of its staff to investigate, and being satisfied with the arrangements there was no way sewage could enter the brook. The Clerk was instructed by the Chairman, William Stops, to tell Gibson that he was misinformed. A further complaint, which was resolved at a later RDC meeting, was the closing of the footpath from Eastcote to Pattishall and use of bicycles by Camp personnel. In the following year, the Clerk reported to the RDC on 21st September that "he had written to H.M. Office of Works….to make a claim in respect of the damage done to the roads by the extraordinary traffic from the Railway Station to the camp at Eastcote." The RDC appears to have had some success, for at its meeting on 2nd November 1915 it was noted that "the Clerk had received and paid into the Bank…£100 in settlement [for damage to the roads] which was considered very satisfactory."

The presence of the Camp continued to present local problems, not least those of movement and access for the residents in the parish. On May 30th 1916 the RDC Clerk informed the members of a letter from Col Fawcett [Assistant Secretary at the War Office] of his intention of "closing the public highway [Bird's Hill Road] between Eastcote and the Infant School on Sundays and not other days as might be necessary." The RDC responded with the proposal "that in special cases passes should be issued to residents in the neighbourhood". At their next meeting in June 1916 the councillors heard that the Commandant was prepared to "issue permits to use the road to certain residents for any day it may be closed if application is made to him."

For what reasons road closures were made is not clear. We can speculate that these could facilitate the movement of drafts of prisoners in and out of the Camp, or for their exercise marching referred to in inspectors' reports. For some Sunday worshippers a closure would require a detour along Pound Lane or around the footpaths linking Eastcote with Pattishall's parish church, or possibly have provided Eastcote's Baptist Chapel with a swollen congregation.

The local press was invariably on the look-out for news. The *Northampton Independent* told its readers on 3rd October 1914:

"The prisoners are accommodated in bell tents and in a large farmhouse on a farm formerly occupied by Mr Gresham…there are at present 50 Germans…but 2,000 are expected next week."

With this news was a photograph (Fig.1.6) with the caption:

"BOY SCOUTS GUARD GERMAN PRISONERS"

Presumably the police with their cutlasses were in support. Improvisation in the face of rapid change was to be a feature of early government responses to the POW question. However, a link had developed between Boy Scouts and public service in times of national crisis and Boy Scouts were utilised at Alton Abbey and other civilian internment camps. At this period the arrangements at Eastcote seem to have been very much on an *ad hoc* basis with the NSFU, the police, and Home Office making decisions as events occurred. The escalating war changed all that and the needs of the military authorities would eventually take precedence. But for the time being Eastcote Camp remained under the watchful eye of the Home Office that, through the DAC, authorised the choice of the civilian Commandant.

In mid-November some of the merchant seamen prisoners were taken from Eastcote to Surrey to the Frith Hill POW Camp (Fig.1.7), but whether to work there, or on their way to the Isle of Man is not clear. In any case, to catch a morning train from Northampton Station on 10th November they were marched into the town on the previous day and spent the night in the local gaol, apparently deemed handy accommodation. A report in the *Northampton Mercury* noted "most of them were of good physical proportions".

The NSFU hosted a joint conference at Eastcote House on 24th November 1914 between thirteen of its own representatives and three from the National Union of Ships' Stewards, Butchers and Bakers to discuss wages in a wartime situation. Seemingly, at this time the NSFU was demonstrating to a fellow union that it owned some pleasant country property, or perhaps it was simply convenient to get away from London for a joint business meeting. At an Executive Council Meeting of the NSFU back in London on 19th December, a question was asked about the finances of the Alton Abbey Camp. As no one was really sure of the arrangements, it was decided to refer the matter to the Finance Committee - although subsequent minutes reveal nothing on this. On the other hand, Wilson declared that the money laid out on Eastcote Camp "was well spent" going, as it was, to the improvement of provision for "our old and disabled members" by whom presumably he meant both the German and Austrian aliens at the Camp - Austria had joined the war on 12th August 1914. It was one of these aliens who, on 30th December 1914, had a letter printed in the *Berliner Tageblatt und Handels-Zeitung*, a German newspaper well-known for its anti-military, anti-imperial and liberal stance, in which he declared how well he was looked after, as we shall see in the next chapter.

Meanwhile, on 14th November, McGhee and Hopkins bought a piece of land (6a.3r.3p.*) in Eastcote for £700 comprising Far Field and Middle Field, from Albert Malsbury of Greenway Farm who also ran a beef-selling business in Kentish Town, London; it was his London address that he used for this transaction. In the following year, on 26th June 1915, McGhee and Hopkins jointly purchased for £250, from Miss Florence Hornsby, another piece of Eastcote land (3a.2r.37p.†), comprising Elm Tree Close (which had been part of glebe land in the previous century) occupied by John William Kingston. These purchases provided the NSFU with the larger area needed around Eastcote House for an expanding POW Camp (Fig.1.8). At this stage we enter a new phase in the history of the Camp.

Whilst in the NSFU surviving ledger of Eastcote House accounts there are numerous and regular payments to Wilson, there are none recorded to McGhee or Hopkins, so we have to assume that they purchased the land in Pattishall themselves for the use of the NSFU, rather than on behalf of the Union. Indeed, as we shall see in Chapter 6, it was they as individuals who, after the war, subsequently sold the land.

---

* 6 acres, 3 roods, 3 perches
† 3 acres, 2 roods, 37 perches

Fig 1.1. Eastcote House, Pattishall (J Lees postcard)

Fig 1.2. 1911 Census return of Eastcote House (The National Archives)

Fig 1.3. Internees at Olympia, 1914 (Illustrated War News)

Fig 1.4. Alton Abbey, Hampshire 2012 (C Chapman)

Fig 1.5. Rev George Gibson,
Vicar of Pattishall 1897-1924 (R Moss)

Fig 1.6. Boy Scouts guarding Eastcote House, 1914 (Northampton Independent)

Fig 1.7. Men marching to Frith Hill Camp, Surrey (C Chapman)

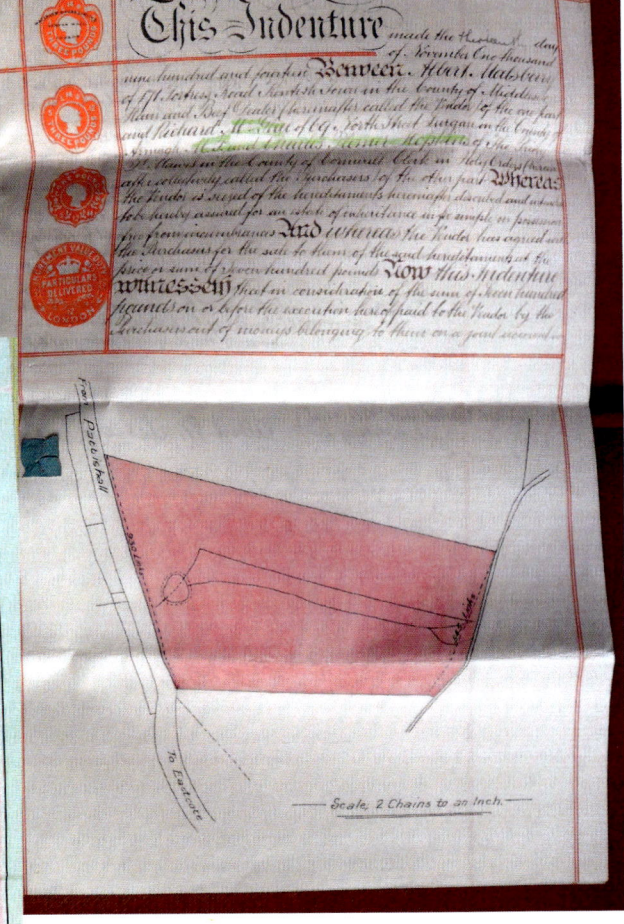

Fig 1.8. Sale of land by Malsbury to Hopkins and McGhee (R Hawtin)

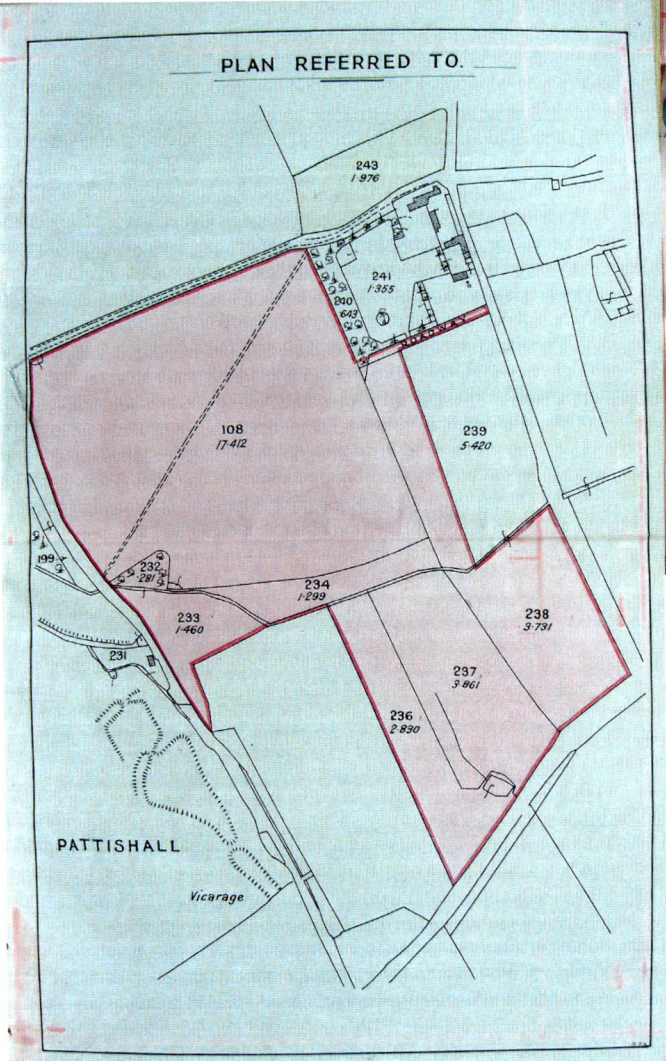

Fig 1.9. Location of Eastcote House in Pattishall (R Hawtin)

2. THE CAMP: Phase I
1914 – 1915

For Joseph Havelock Wilson, the first year of the Camp was the best in every respect. Some three years later, in November 1917, he had an opportunity to express his feelings to Howard Marshall of *The Observer*. Wilson, "a plain sailor"….."who can never be anything more than an A.B.", related:

"Before the War, German seamen had great opportunities for employment upon British ships. [They were often preferred, being] sober and more attentive to their duties…there was no bad feeling between British and German seafaring men before the war began. At the outbreak of the war we British members of the Union were sorry for the Germans… and …. we sympathised with those whom our government felt it necessary to intern….

The British Seamen's [sic] and Firemen's Union begged that those Germans who were members of the corresponding German Union should be interned in a camp which was under the control of the Union, and greatly to its credit, the British government quickly consented to this evidence of our fraternal feeling. So in a lovely district near Northampton, a splendid place for Interned men was established."

Warming to his subject in the reflective glow of retrospection he gave details of the Camp as he recalled it:

"At one time it had about a thousand inmates. They had wooden huts to sleep in and four good meals a day. The only guards were fourteen policemen, who were never allowed actually to enter the Camp. They had concert halls, cinema shows, and all kinds of musical entertainments. They had bottled beer three times a week, and each was given four ounces of tobacco every seven days. It was mighty polite, and fine imprisonment, which they were called upon to endure – imprisonment far more comfortable than any freedom they ever had known."

There was some substance in Wilson's comments. In January 1915 the *Northampton Daily News* published a translation of a letter, supposedly from a German seaman interned in the Camp, sent to the *Berliner Tageblatt* in December 1914.

Nov 17 1914

"The establishment of the Camp is as follows – A large tent holding between 800 and 900 men serves as a dining tent…heated by 6 large slow-combustion stoves…a kitchen and a… bakery…clean and practical…The food is good…we sleep at present in smaller tents, 8 to 10 men in each…when darkness sets in the whole camp is brilliantly lighted. A wash house with cold and warm water and 12 shower baths is in the course of being built…also another large tent for a reading and writing room (English and German literature is available)…The Commandant is not pleased with the tents for sleeping and intends to have wooden huts built. The guarding of the camp is in the hands of civil authorities. We possess a shoemaker's shop, where everyone can have boots repaired free of charge. Working clothes and bedding are served out to those who have none. Those who work in the kitchen and those who act as waiting receive a small sum each week...The building of the camp is in the hands of the inmates. All receive 3 issues a week of cigarettes or tobacco and beer. There is a hospital with a doctor and nurses on hand"

The writer finished by stating how friendly "the natives of our village" were and hoped that British POWs would receive the same generous treatment as he had. At this stage there was no independent inspection of POW camps managed by either Germany or Britain, and in spite of testimonies provided by letters such as this, rumours circulated in both countries of the harsh treatment of captives and internees leading to retaliatory measures being taken. To obviate such retaliation the American Ambassador in Berlin had been negotiating since early November 1914 for US attachés to undertake inspections of the POW camps, and for reports on these to be exchanged between the embassies in London and Berlin, to be transmitted to the British and German governments, with copies to be sent also to the ICRC in Geneva. The first permit given to the US Embassy in London was issued on 27th January 1915 for a complete inspection of all the POW camps in the UK. The comprehensive report filed at the US Embassy in Berlin on 27th February made no mention of Eastcote, as at that time it was still very much within the NSFU's domain. On 17th March 1915, the German Government accepted independent inspections of its camps holding British prisoners.

Worried about the increasing costs of maintaining the Eastcote Camp, Wilson wrote on 18th February 1915 to David Lloyd George, at that time Chancellor of the Exchequer, seeking an interview to explain the situation. Being an MP, Wilson perhaps felt that a direct approach to the man holding the purse strings would be more fruitful. But Lloyd George chose to pass the concerns to Reginald McKenna, the Home Secretary. Hence, on 25th February 1915 Wilson and Charles Bowerman - Labour MP for Deptford - met the Home Secretary to seek an increase from the 10/- a week per man allowance. In a follow-up letter to McKenna on 5th March, Wilson pointed out that the real cost was 11/7½d. The Union had spent £5,600 fitting out the Camp, exclusive of the cost of buying the land. He asked for an additional 1/- per man "during the continuance of the present figures" (which at that time totalled 289 men in the Camp). In Parliament, Bowerman sought from the government comparable figures for the camps on the Isle of Man and for the nine ships moored at Ryde, Portsmouth and Southend, being used temporarily to house POWs. In a written reply it was revealed that the weekly cost on the Isle of Man stood at 10/- (precisely the sum the government was allowing at Eastcote), and it was expected that by mid-April the nine ships would be released for other government services. On 27/28th March the NSFU Executive Council moved their regret that the Destitute Aliens' Committee was unable to recommend the extra 1/- per man per week, but notwithstanding reaffirmed their determination to keep the Camp running.

On 30th April 1915 a Parliamentary delegation visited the Camp and found it "a very different place from the score of military camps previously visited." The party comprised Sir Ryland Adkins, Sir Henry Dalziel and Messrs P O'Brien, G H Roberts, E A Strauss, G Stewart and W T Wilson. Selected extracts from their findings, after other camp visits, were reported in *The Times* on 13th May. The visitors were in a quandary as to whom the Eastcote Camp was answerable. "The War Office has nothing to do with it". To them it seemed to be the joint creation of Havelock Wilson, the Seamen's [*sic*] and Firemen's Union and the Destitute Aliens' Committee. Wilson was running the Camp and employed a Commandant who was neither a soldier nor police officer but claimed to be under the Home Office. [We know, however, from files in The National Archives that the DAC had appointed the Commandant by early October 1914.] Although "The camp is guarded by nine members of the Northampton County Constabulary", the MPs commented in 1915, "It did not appear…that there was much to prevent any man escaping if he wished to do so."

That such an event had already occurred (see Chapter 4) concerned the delegates. More so, as the individual had made his way to the east coast and taken a job on a North Sea collier that provided fuel to British naval ships. When the culprit was caught and returned, the Eastcote Commandant refused to have him back. We have not been able to discover the culprit's name or to where he was sent.

The delegation's report continues: "the property…consists of a medium-sized house….and 60 acres of agricultural land [that were bought for] about £3,500; 27 acres of the land are enclosed in a high fence put up by the Home Office [for] about £500". There were 779 inmates at the time of their visit for which "The Government pays the union 10s. a head a week".

The quality of the men was commented upon by the MPs: "…in many instances very fine men. A good many …. are old sailors and they all seemed as happy as could be." The sailors found incarceration less of a hardship than landsmen. "They have plenty to eat and nothing to do, and plenty of elbow-room to move about in."

The MPs admired both "the little model port" that the men had constructed with "model ships of all kinds…..with model wharves, cranes and piers" showing that "the inmates have a great fund of ingenuity", and also "the great number of neat and artistic garden plots" and the beginnings of "a large swimming bath in the park." (Figs. 2.1, 2.2, 2.3). They defined the Camp as a detention centre rather than a place of internment. It did appear, in army terms, to be 'a cushy billet'. One villager from Astcote, Ron Liddington, recalled that some of the men were allowed out on occasions, such as to visit the local Mop or Hiring Fair, better known as Booth Statis or Statute Fair, at nearby Foster's Booth – although, as this fair was held every September, he may have been remembering a period when conditions were more relaxed after the Versailles Treaty of 1919.

Sadly, these idyllic scenarios and rose-tinted recollections proved short-lived, as events beyond Eastcote Camp were to have a dramatic impact on its fortunes. Although parts of the MPs' report appeared in *The Times* on 13th May, these obviously reflected the situation in the Camp observed by the MPs at the end of April, otherwise surely there would have been some mention of the complete swing in empathy to the POWs by both Wilson and his NSFU colleagues following a major international incident on 7th May 1915. On that fateful day, some 11 miles off the Irish Coast, the German submarine U-20 torpedoed *RMS Lusitania*; nearly 1,200 of the 1,960 men, women and children on board were drowned, so changing the hearts and minds of very many British citizens (Fig.2.4).

Wilson described the response within the Camp to this news in his interview with Marshall from *The Observer* some two-and-a-half years later:
"A concert had been organised…the Germans were called together, and I explained to them that we would suspend the concert for a time, out of respect for the five hundred of our fellow-members who had been done to death…. There were about a thousand Germans in the hall…and when I stopped there was dead silence…I was scarcely outside the door before the men began to sing 'The Watch on the Rhine' and other German patriotic songs. Presently the singing gave place to cheers."

Captain Edward Tupper, his close friend, recalled how Wilson was devastated by the behaviour of the Germans in the Camp theatre (Fig.2.5). Here were fellow-seamen to whom he had comradely devoted much of his life and this was how they showed their fellowship.

Tupper wrote: "Wilson stood as though turned to stone. His face, always pain-racked and wan, looked ghastly under the moon. I have never in my life seen any man's face change in a moment as his changed then. It appalled me. He gripped my arm, and I saw moonlight glittering on the tears streaming down his face." [Ref.2.1].

Tupper recalling drama as he saw it, continued: " Skipper," Wilson gasped, "take me up to the house"… I stood by his chair [into which he had collapsed], and he gripped my hand. "Ted," he said, "…I always thought we were at war with Pan-Prussian Military Party. Now I know we are at war with the German people." Tupper moved from the graphic change in Wilson to the rapid resolution, blissfully short-circuiting the historical realities: "He told me to 'phone the Home Office that he would be there at ten. We were, and the Seamen's [sic] Union washed their hands of the whole thing…Within a few hours the German seamen at Eastcote saw barbed wire going up around them, and soon bayonets were gleaming beyond the wire". The smaller camp at Alton Abbey had already closed in April.

On 20th May 1915 Wilson composed a letter to Sir William Byrne, Chairman of the DAC. It was brisk, businesslike and to the point, namely the potential transfer of the management of Eastcote Camp from the NSFU to the War Office. Wilson gave his reasons – the 60 acre site was close to roads, rail and the Weedon Barracks (Fig.2.6), it had the capacity to hold 5,000 to 6,000, possibly 8,000 POWs, and had a sufficient water supply for even 10,000. The landfall suited additional sewerage and sanitation. Materials were close at hand; possibly he had in mind the quarry near Dalscote [see pages 24 and 42]. He set out two possible arrangements: firstly a camp on 8-acre and 17-acre fields for 5,000 to 6,000 men, leaving 35 acres for additional accommodation and recreation. Secondly he suggested, though clearly did not favour, the creation of four isolated compounds. In the event the latter option was chosen.

"…. All that would be required to carry on the work of construction would be a suitable man such as we have already had for the last 8 months and one or two good leading men, whom we have already had….."

Wilson was ensuring that contract work would go to those he already employed on the staff. He undertook to put these proposals to the NSFU Finance Committee. The Union's interests (or interests of its trustees) in the freehold property at Eastcote were presumably to be retained despite the intended transfer to War Office control. The letter demonstrates how much Wilson had invested of his time and commitment to the Camp. It was at the heart of his life and he played a pivotal part in its inception as a place of refuge for merchant seamen.

Looking back in November 1917 at the May 1915 incident, Wilson poured vitriol upon the prisoners at Eastcote and those who fought the war. So incensed was he in 1917 that during that November he set up a Merchant Seamen's League, open to every citizen of the British Empire, not just mariners, whose members pledged to refuse to employ Germans or purchase or use German goods for two years after the war. His aspiration was to recruit five million members, each paying an annual subscription of a shilling. In fact, it was Wilson's formation of the League as well as his award of a CBE that caused Marshall to interview him for *The Observer* article from which we have quoted earlier in this chapter.

Shortly after the concert debacle in May 1915 there were further disorderly incidents amongst the prisoners which the Commandant had difficulty bringing under control. The MPs, however, only a week earlier had drawn attention to the relaxed and easy nature of guarding the Camp, albeit with the potential for escape. How drastically the situation had changed!

The scale and the impact of the war, public outcry against Germans and Zeppelin raids in June, rising casualty lists which affected all sections of society, and the presence in Eastcote Camp of military combatants along with civilian internees, added to the pressure on men such as Wilson, Hopkins and McGhee. Indeed, Wilson's change of heart was part of this change as well as a cause. Between May 1915 and June 1916, with authority passing to the War Office, the Camp was transformed somewhat along the lines Wilson had suggested. But the growth of Eastcote, with the potential to hold up to 10,000 POWs, was modest by comparison with Knockaloe Camp on the Isle of Man constructed in the same period to ultimately house 23,000.

At a meeting of the NSFU Executive Council in London on 25th September 1915, Wilson informed those present that "the connection between Union and the camp would cease on October 11th". Phase I in the life of Eastcote Camp was about to draw to a close.

Fig 2.1. Model harbour with POWs (J Lees postcard)

Fig 2.2. POWs tending gardens (ICRC postcard)

Fig 2.3. Model harbour with sailing boats (J Lees postcard)

Fig 2.4. RMS Lusitania commemorative medal (C Chapman)

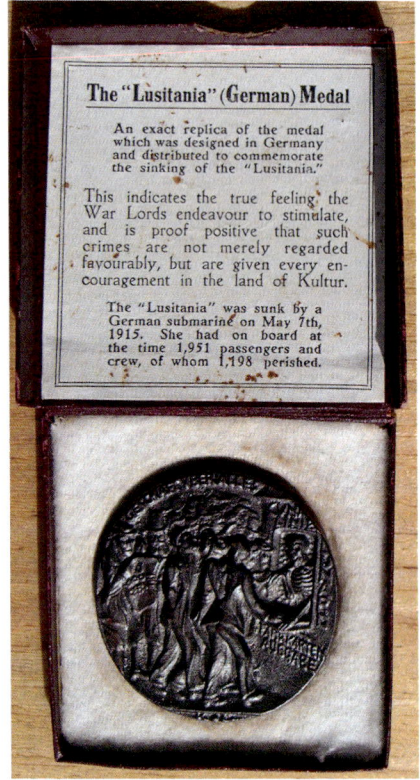

Fig 2.5. Interior of camp theatre (1916 book)

3. THE CAMP: Phase II
1915 – 1920

The War Office took over control of Eastcote Camp on 11th October 1915 under the terms of DORA (Defence of the Realm Act, 1914). A photograph in the Mary Evans Archive [Ref.3.1] depicts Eastcote Camp in the process of expansion and refurbishment with the reservoir under construction. Two men are at work on fencing. The photographer in 1915 was standing on the slope about 100 metres to the north east of the reservoir taking the slightly blurred image. Robert Hawtin remembers helping his father Henry remove elms pictured in a line left of centre, which remain as marks on the ground to-day. In December 1915, at short notice according to a Quaker report, all the internees were moved temporarily to Alexandra Palace in north London while Eastcote Camp was enlarged and refurbished.

Between May 1915 and May 1919 Alexandra Palace was often used as a short-term holding camp for POWs in transit; many from there were soon removed to the Isle of Man as accommodation became available at Douglas and Knockaloe, near Peel. However, civilian internees whose wives lived in the London area remained at the Palace for much of the war to facilitate regular visiting by their spouses. Some of the men at the Palace were seen by one who termed himself "a neutral writer" in his account in *The Times* on 21st December 1915. He described over 2,000 internees including, we presume, the Eastcote contingent, who appeared well-fed, liked their Commandant and were entertaining themselves in music and drama.

The Eastcote internees did not stay long at Alexandra Palace, for they were back by 2nd February 1916 when Edward Lowry from the American Embassy visited Eastcote Camp. The hasty removal and swift return of the men may have contributed to some missing luggage, to which we refer below. The February visit was the first occasion on which Eastcote Camp was officially inspected under the terms agreed between Britain and Germany in the early part of 1915. It is from reports such as this, rather than from correspondence written by the POWs themselves, that we may gain an impression of what the Camp was like. As we shall see in Chapter 6, prisoners' letters generally touched only on the monotony of time and place, relieved from time to time when they went out on working parties or to satellite camps further afield.

From the first American report compiled in February 1916 we learn the Camp contained 600 Germans and 60 Austrians. Virtually all of the internees were sailors (Fig.3.1). They had a new Commandant, Lt. Col. John Henry Ansley formerly of the North Lancashire Regt. He had retired in 1913 but was brought back into service initially as Commandant at Lancaster POW Camp in 1914 and moved to Eastcote in 1916 when he was 53. The POWs, as in most other camps, had organised themselves on the lines of two committees, named Markel and Lowry after their philanthropic instigators. There were four 4-acre compounds, though only one was in use, with five sleeping huts per compound. Lowry gives us their dimensions: the huts were 200ft x 30ft x 12ft 6ins. Each, lit by electricity, slept three units of men with three stoves per hut, the wooden bunks standing 18 inches above the floor (Fig.3.2). Every prisoner had four blankets and a straw palliasse. Each compound had a 22-compartment latrine, a bathhouse with 44 basins and 10 shower baths with hot and cold running water. A steam-heated room specifically to dry washing, and an incinerator also featured in each compound. Running piped water from a spring, which fed 80,000 gallons per day, was pumped through filters into a reservoir built by the prisoners. A later deed of 1923 defined the respective rights to the common water supply for the house and drainage of land, and an accompanying map shows the layout of the pipework to Eastcote House, the cottage, stables and a single-storey house, possibly used as the Camp nurses' accommodation. We may note here that the spring had its source under the fields of Sand's Farm at Foster's Booth. To the best of Robert Hawtin's and his father's knowledge (who have subsequently farmed the fields where the Camp stood), it has never stopped flowing nor ever frozen up, and the water was fit for drinking both then and now.

The February 1916 report mentions an infirmary sited in a third of one of the huts. It had 16 beds, two doctors, one German and four British attendants. A large, fully equipped, hospital under construction was to house two ward-wings each with 36 beds. An isolation hospital was also being prepared. There was a camp kitchen with 12 cooks and bakers who used 8 double ranges, 4 boilers and a baking oven (Fig.3.3). There were two storerooms. The former daily issue of 1½lbs bread for each prisoner had been replaced by 1lb bread and 6ozs of flour that they could use to make cakes, pastry or use however they chose.

A recreation hut and workshop, built by the men themselves was 100ft long, 8ft high and 18ft wide and it was noted they were very pleased with it. No work seemed to be organised for the prisoners (Fig.3.4) although a Quaker Committee had been set up to encourage industrial work such as toy-making. There were no teachers and no educational classes. A nine-acre playing field was set aside and in use. When Lowry spoke to the men he received a request from a 57-year old prisoner for repatriation. Three others voiced concerns for their English wives. Several complained that when they returned from Alexandra Palace some of their personal belongings were missing. Security was much heightened with the replacement of civilian guards by military personnel. When completed, Lowry reported, the Camp would have the capacity to take 4,000 POWs but it was already in a good condition.

On 11th April 1916 the Camp was inspected again by an attaché from the American Embassy, on this occasion by Boylston A Beal. Its population was much increased; there were 1,559 men in total comprising 854 civilian and 705 military personnel, of whom 749 were Germans, 95 Austrians, 5 Turkish and 5 others. Two of the 4-acre compounds were now in use, one for the combatant prisoners, the other for the civilian internees. The combatant POWs had a German *Feldwebel-Leutnant* [equivalent to a Company Sergeant Major, the highest ranking NCO in the German army during the Great War] leading them, while the civilians had a German Camp Captain as their head. All the POWs expressed "confidence and respect for the Camp Commandant Lt. Col. J. H. Ansley and the officers of the guard". The prisoners had organised their own committees for administering/organising the Kitchen, Athletics and Sports, Bands, Choral and Drama activities and a School.

None of the POWs "seem inclined to do much work...some were engaged in carpentry, path and bag-making". For all work that was done, other than fatigues, the prisoners were paid. Beal hoped that with the completion of the Camp the men might take a more positive approach to doing something, although they did seem to take pride in the creation of a network of neat pathways throughout the Camp. "A large building is almost ready for a theatre or Concert Hall", Beal reported. In addition, prisoners were taken out on route marches and were provided with gymnastic equipment and a recreation field of 9-acres for football and other games. There were still complaints about the loss of effects occasioned while they were housed temporarily at Alexandra Palace.

The new hospital had been completed but was still unfurnished, so sick prisoners remained lodged in the temporary hospital as in February. There were 19 in-patients including two soldiers, and 40 out-patients five of whom were soldiers suffering from "chronic nervousness, colds and rheumatism". Some prisoners who had been transferred from the Dalston

German Hospital in east London complained that they had been discharged from there before they had fully recovered. Each compound, accommodating four companies of 50 men, had its own kitchen. As all companies were allocated either a German or Austrian cook, both compounds saw 20 cooks busy at work. Sanitation was carefully monitored and found to be in good order.

Beal found the Camp well administered; there was only one man in the cells for gross insubordination whom Beal felt had no grounds to complain about the accommodation which was "clean, dry, well-warmed and well lighted." The American Inspector clearly saw much progress and considerable potential for the Camp. It was perhaps just as well.

It is not surprising that construction was still incomplete. Snowfalls earlier in the year had made an impact, as the Log Book for the Pattishall Village School records:
"March 28th 1916: A very heavy fall of snow again this morning. The Head Teacher came to school but no children came so as the snow was very deep & still falling she closed the school for the day." "March 30th: A record snow storm on Tuesday afternoon has completely isolated the various villages & neither teachers nor scholars were able to get to school on Wednesday. Today the Assistant Teacher (Miss Margaret Miller) opened school as the Head Teacher was unable to attend through illness, but was obliged to close again as only 3 children were present in the morning and also in the afternoon." [Ref.3.2]

On 2nd September 1916 Francis E Brantingham, an attaché from the American Embassy, visited Frith Hill Camp at Frimley near Aldershot. In his report he stated:
"…the present camp, opened July 17 1916…is a working camp formed of POWs brought from Eastcote to build a railway in the vicinity. The prisoners number 1499 all Germans of whom 1441 are military and 58 naval prisoners…Some 14 POWs complained through their spokesman, Wilhelm Brauckhoff, POW No. 247, that they were Red Cross men and desired to be repatriated as such. The case of these men has been brought to the attention of the War Office."

Under the terms of the Geneva and Hague Conventions the United Kingdom was required to repatriate all Red Cross personnel captured. The Foreign and Home Offices agreed, but the War Office dragged its feet. Although Lord Kitchener had drowned in June 1916 and Lloyd George had replaced him as Secretary of State for War, his dictum lived on, that it was unacceptable to send Germans back to nurse our enemy's wounded. In practice, General William Robertson, with direct access to the Cabinet, now ran the War Office, but little progress on this and similar issues was made during the war.

During 1916 the British Government initiated the practice of establishing satellite working camps dependent on parent POW camps. Precisely how this system was administered at this time is not clear (we know of the 1918 arrangements) but seemingly there were about a dozen major parent camps throughout Britain, having working camps or agricultural depots with reasonable access to rail and road links. The working camps served two purposes: offering accommodation for the ever-expanding POW numbers in parent camps, as more and more men were captured as the war progressed, whilst also providing much needed labour for agriculture, forestry, quarrying, fen clearance etc., according to local needs - the British labour force had become severely depleted by men serving abroad. Some parent camps covered very large areas: Stobs Camp in Roxburghshire, for example, was the parent for all of Scotland and had at least one satellite in Lincolnshire. Eastcote initially took responsibility for a few camps in the immediate locality; but as we shall see, by the end of the war, looked after the POW working camps in 13 counties in an area to the south and east of a line drawn roughly from the Wash through Rutland to the Isle of Wight – the area under the British army's 'Eastern Command'. By January 1919, according to a POWIB printed list, there were 144 satellites, including 124 working camps, 14 agricultural groups, (largely in East Anglia), 5 agricultural depots (specifically identified, although another seven places are named as depots, groups and working camps). There was also a civilian working camp at Corby, associated with the ironstone workings, though its administration was for much of the war handled from Knockaloe. Details on inspections of, escapes from, a truck accident and a death from choking over food at, the Corby POW camp are described in Chapman's fuller account of the satellite camps associated with Pattishall – see Bibliography.

In 1916, three weeks after his inspection of Frith Hill Camp, Brantingham visited Eastcote Camp on 22nd September. Significantly, he reported that all 854 civilian internees had been transferred to other camps in July 1916, and stated "The camp is now exclusively military". He does not report that the four compounds for the POWs were now in use, compared with only two of them in April, but we know this from a letter written by one of the POWs in May 1916 – see Chapter 5. In 1916 much had taken place in the world of war outside the Camp. The Battle of the Somme on 1st July left appalling casualties and many POWs were taken by both sides. The removal of the civilian prisoners in July was perhaps no coincidence. When Brantingham checked numbers during this September inspection there were 1,448 prisoners of whom 33 were naval and 1,415 military. He added that a further 298 former internees had been moved to forestry working camps: 131 at Woburn in Bedfordshire and 167 at Panshanger in Hertfordshire. We should recall that two years before, in August 1914, there had been 779 POWs, all civilians – the original German merchant seamen. Later reports show that in May 1917 there were 2,043 combatant POWs (1,994 army and 49 naval) with a further 1,600 at twelve working camps and in October 1917, as we shall see, the parent Camp alone housed 3,493 POWs of whom 42 were sailors.

In September 1916, Brantingham found the two wards of the camp hospital had been furnished since the previous (April) inspection, with 36 beds in each and 8 beds in the isolation hospital. The seven medical staff comprised two doctors, five British soldiers from the RAMC and two German attendants. The POWs' spiritual needs were met by a British Roman Catholic priest attending the Camp once a fortnight to hold mass and hear confessions, although it seems to us that the Protestants fared rather better, as a visiting German pastor came every Tuesday to hold services in the recreation hut. The theatre and concert hall had been completed and was now in regular use, and the Camp lit throughout by electricity from the camp's own generator. It may be significant to comment here that Pattishall's parishioners had to wait until the 1930s before the village was supplied with electricity and the decision to install street lighting was not made until 1950.

Brantingham spoke to around twenty-five of the POWs during his visit; from his report we unusually discover the identity of one of the NCOs, Fähnrich von Schweinichen, and also that two Red Cross men originated from German overseas territories in South-West Africa and the Cameroons, possibly Pattishall's first black parishioners. Mark [Ref.3.3] tells us that von Schweinichen had previously been in Dorchester POW Camp in Dorset and in Woking Detention Barracks as a result of trying to escape from Stobs POW Camp in Scotland.

The Camp with the model port was now the setting for the grim arithmetic of warfare, yet Brantingham found the prisoners "mostly contented with conditions... well clothed... strong and in good health." They were housed in 200ft long huts with windows at intervals, between bed spaces. The NCOs had their own quarters and the other ranks theirs. They had fish in lieu of meat once a week, route marches for 300 men at a time four times a week, and physical exercise for one hour a day with their own instructors. The nature of the wounded suggests that some had come directly from the battlefield – for it was strongly recommended that all amputees should be transferred to other hospitals.

Brantingham's report of his visit on 22nd September 1916 throws a little light on the situation in the POW Camp at Pattishall: men were marched into the fields on farms in the parish and adjacent parishes. Subsequent oral recall refers to POWs assembled on the green at Astcote where the children pulled tongues at them. We have photographs of men at work at Descote quarry, Dalscote [see page 42]. Others worked in Northampton; an elderly lady recalled to a correspondent that prisoners were marched into the town to work there but in bad weather, rather than march back, they were billeted overnight in the cellars of a dry-cleaning shop in Weedon Road, and returned to the Camp later [Ref.3.4].

Leisure activities included drama, music, football, model-making and occasional outings of two kinds: route marches twice weekly and social. According to Miss E M Wilson whose uncle kept *The Boot Inn* on Gayton Road, Eastcote where she stayed for her holidays:

"I would be about 7...My cousin and I used to walk by the prison camp and, through the wire, we could see the prisoners walking about. Kids like we used to put our tongues out at them. They were allowed out with a warden for a walk to the end of the village, to where my uncle's inn was and have a pint or two. Sometimes my uncle's small son would be stood on a stool and sing to the prisoners. He was only 4 years old. He would sing 'Old Soldiers Never Die, they only fade away'. They would give him coppers to put in his money box." [Ref.3.5].

Allowing POWs under escort a stroll to the nearest local, rather than to work, suggests that Miss Wilson was staying at *The Boot* after 1918 or much earlier in the more relaxed regime of the NSFU Camp. However, it is clear from other memories that the villagers did not have strong antipathies to the prisoners, some of whom stayed with families in neighbouring farms – but again this was may have been later in the life of the Camp, probably after the Armistice or even after the Treaty of Versailles in 1919.

The presence of combatant prisoners in thousands required complex safety measures. Long gone were the tents and marquees and the cheerful improvisation of the first six months in the Camp's history. Some idea of what was utilised can be found in the advertisement for the post-war sale of effects which appeared the *Northampton Mercury* on 19th March 1920. Details of access to the sale referred to the close proximity of Northampton (6 miles), Blisworth Junction of the London and North Eastern Railway (4 miles) and Towcester (3 miles).

Firstly the barbed wire – 66 tons of it; besides this - fencing 2,600 feet of 8ft weatherboarding and 19 observation boxes up to 70ft long on 10ft high timber stands, formerly at intervals around the perimeter. Presumably the military authorities had removed the arc-lights and other security fixtures following the final evacuation of POWs from the Camp in late 1919. There were 24 sleeping huts 200ft x 30ft and 4,200 bedboards, cookhouses, ablution rooms, drying rooms, a flour store 55ft x 25ft, a brick and glass bakehouse with 8 ovens, four 60ft x 15ft timber and weatherboard huts, together with a ten-roomed insulated administrative block 73ft x 36ft completely fitted throughout. A brick-built electric generating station and two boiler houses had evidently provided power and hot water. Water and sanitation came from a 2,751,500 gallon concrete reservoir, and a sewage system of septic tanks, filter beds and sprinklers. There were baths, sinks, hot water pipes, electric wiring, cooking ranges, boilers and heating stoves. A complete hospital system, installed in 1916, was also for sale with two wards fitted throughout, medical officers' rooms, an isolation hospital and an "excellent five-roomed sectional bungalow on brick foundations". The 48 cupboards and 235 tables could have served for writing desks on which the prisoners wrote their letters home. From inspection reports we know that the roadways inside the Camp were surfaced in places with railway sleepers – 3,500 of these were in the sale. Corrugated iron sheets also suggest other materials were utilised to assist traction for wheeled traffic or perhaps roofing. We have to assume that all the buildings were left *in situ* for the prospective purchasers to view - but more of the 1920 sale in Chapter 6.

The appearance of the Camp while in use can be further deduced from a few surviving photographs that we have obtained from various sources. Some were taken and published in about 1915 as a set of four postcards by Jonathan Lees, the locally-respected wholesale tobacconist and picture framer in Northampton. A Christmas postcard for 1916 with German greetings has scenes of POWs with model sailing boats on the camp reservoir and a football match in progress with a row of huts in the background; a superimposed football is high in the sky - perhaps a symbol of the freedom they all wished for (Fig.3.5). 17 pictures of the Camp appear in an undated, but probably 1916, book of photographs, taken at the request of the American Ambassador in Berlin by the Photographic Section of the Royal Flying Corps, showing the camps at Donington Hall, Alexandra Palace, Dorchester, Handforth, Lofthouse Park and Eastcote (Fig.3.6). Copies of all of the photographs could be purchased by the POWs held in the camps. These photographs are extremely useful since they illustrate many camp scenes. At Eastcote, for example, we can see men inside a hut having twenty 'pull-down' windows on each side, a group of prisoners standing before a background of a double row of barbed-wire fencing, beyond which is a field and a hedge running alongside Banbury Lane; the theatre, the bakery, the carpenters' shop, the gardens and huts are all clearly depicted. Two cards were issued in early 1917 by the ICRC as part of a series of 37 picture postcards of British POW Camps; on one of these the prisoners at Pattishall tend their 'allotment gardens', as described in inspection reports, while the other shows men beside their hand-made watermill and model merry-go-round.

There are also unofficial photographs, a few of which have been fortuitously drawn to our attention, taken by the prisoners themselves as mementos to keep or to send to their friends and relatives. An attractive one from Alf Krauplatz, POW No.12640, of Hut 340 addressed to Frau Linette Krauplatz, perhaps his wife, in Meiningen, shows him standing in his uniform alongside one of the rows of wooden huts (Fig.3.7). Another, from Andreas Bartmann, POW No.18709 from Hut 1440, sent to Frauline Mari Gillitzer in Bavaria, depicts five men in uniform (two holding cigarettes) in the grounds, standing behind an occasional table covered with a fancy cloth on which there is pot and some cut flowers. Unfortunately, neither of these cards is dated. Another photograph, written on 23rd July 1916 by Emil Stöckl, POW No.3943, and sent to his girlfriend Marie Höflings in Nürnberg, shows a performance in action in the camp theatre (Fig.3.8). In his message he mentions that G Reinhold, a family friend who has been wounded, is a fellow POW at Pattishall.

Whilst no detailed plan of the Camp has yet been found, the picture postcards and photographs give some idea of the lay-out, although the precise location of the buildings remains conjectural. However, when Austin Nightingale was building his house beside the lane that served as the main route into the Camp, he came across the basement of the boiler house - a great sunken rectangle - at his feet. Robert Hawtin has studied the topography over many years in winter, spring and summer for crop marks and any traces of foundations. He has suggested a layout as it might have been, incorporating the given areas of each compound as identified by Wilson in 1915. Some of the features are based on objects that have been retrieved at the site over the years – for example a sentry box pulled from Eastcote Brook in the 1920s.

Towards the end of 1916 the name of the Camp was formally changed from Eastcote to Pattishall Camp, possibly because another POW camp at Eastcote in Middlesex bore the same name. The Camp was inspected on 12th May 1917, not on this occasion by a neutral power but seemingly to glean information primarily for Parliament, as R H D Acland and Col Charles Anstruther were the two men involved. As their report was received at the Home Office on 23rd May, the date of 16th August at its foot is obviously a typing error. The report mentioned that the ample quantity of meat the visitors saw on the dining tables for the POWs "did not look very appetising" though they did append a full page of the nature and quantity of rations available. They found "plenty of warm – not hot – water is available for the shower baths" and there was a "very cheerful looking attendant who helps the cripples, of whom there are a very large number in the camp, to bathe themselves" in six bath tubs. The inspectors noted "A dentist (a prisoner) has a small operating room – or hut rather – and as we went by, his operations were being watched through the window by a number of interested spectators". Reference is made to the tangible support given by Dr Markel and the Friends Emergency Committee in the form of musical instruments, wood and tools to undertake carvings and fancy work, and to assistance available in subsequently selling these goods inside and beyond the Camp.

On 16th May 1917 Dr Fritz Schwyzer from the Swiss Legation visited Pattishall. America had joined Britain and her allies in opposing Germany and hers, and so US Embassy officials could no longer act as neutral visiting inspectors. A new Commandant had been appointed at the end of April, Lt. Col O'Donnell Colley Grattan DSO formerly of the Liverpool Regt aged 62, from a well-known Anglo-Irish family. Ansley, Grattan's predecessor, had moved to take over Leigh Camp in Lancashire. The second-in-command was Major F E Foulger, with Dr A J Turner as the Medical Officer. There were additionally three officer interpreters who also acted as the camp censors. Grattan was assisted by members of the Royal Defence Corps and senior NCOs brought back from retirement to assist in 'the war effort'. A photograph shows eight of them (Fig.3.9), all well past active service, seated in front of bay windows, perhaps of Eastcote House. In army parlance they would have been 'old sweats' who would probably have served in India and other territories of the British Empire. From a postcard we know the name of at least one of the Royal Defence Corps, for when 44714 Pte Ed Ogborn was transferred in early 1918 from Pattishall to Kimbolton Castle, one of its satellite camps, he wrote home to Clapham, south London, asking that his clean washing be sent to his new address. From another card we also know that the guards were denied beer while on duty, for Wal (his surname eludes us) wrote to Mrs Bone, the landlady of his east London pub, wishing he could enjoy "a tankard of bitter" with her and his Clapton drinking friends.

Schwyzer, in an unusually long report of eight pages with a further page identifying the POWs' daily rations, helpfully gives us more details on the Camp layout. Each of the four compounds was 90 yds by 130 yds separated from each other by a cross-roads and barbed wire fences. "The ground is stoney and very uneven. Streets and paths, partly board walks, have been built all through the camp." Each compound had a canteen and a small restaurant. However, the range of menus was "crippled through the new food regulations, as they are not allowed to sell anything containing sugar, flour and meat." To add to that constraint, "Alcoholic drinks are not allowed in the camp." What a contrast to the days of NSFU management of the Camp when each of the thousand or so men was permitted three bottles of beer a week! Although each compound had an area set aside for recreation such as fistball or athletics, there was now no large sports field for football or hockey as had been illustrated on the Christmas 1916 postcard.

A hospital compound and a small isolation compound had been added to one of the four compounds since the previous inspection [by a neutral power] in September 1916. Dr Turner, in charge of the hospital, had a British assistant plus eight British and two German orderlies. Three German dentists worked in the Camp and a British dentist visited when needed. The report added: "The German dentists are awaiting impatiently the erection of a small hut where they can prepare plates for artificial teeth and protheses [sic] for a number of men who have injured jaws." This facility had been paid for from 'Markel' funds. There were: "about 33 men now [in the hospital], a great many with old wounds, bomb splinters, injured bones etc, while there are quite a number of men with amputated legs and arms, the stumps of which are not quite healed yet." Further: "since the opening of the camp six cases of lunacy have been sent to the asylum and since January 1st, four." Serious medical cases were sent to Dartford War Hospital, mental cases to Crowthorne.

Work inside Pattishall Camp, beyond the usual fatigue duties, was very limited. Shoemaking, hairdressing and tailoring were sited in workshops and there was also a building set aside for woodcarving and cabinet-making [probably provided by the Quakers], supervised by several skilled cabinet-workers. They made letter stands, paper knives and little boxes. We have seen some of these, still cherished today, that were later given to local parishioners as parting gifts. Some POWs had taken up bookbinding and watch-making. Their creative talents were met through orchestras and music lessons. Each compound had its own theatre, and Schwyzer watched a rehearsal of 'Old Heidleberg'. There were libraries holding 2,750 books in total, where English newspapers could be read. The drafting of six professional teachers to satellite working camps had put a stop to some of the educational projects - a source of complaint from the men to the inspector.

Schwyzer made special reference to the needs of disabled POWs: "There are about seventy badly crippled men in Pattishall: 42 men with only one leg, 27 men with only one arm and 1 man with only one leg and one arm. They have practically no care in this camp…There are, further, a number of men with shattered jaw-bones, who are unable to eat properly." This aspect of the report was seized on with relish by the Germans who included it under the heading "Illegal Offences" on page 15 in the 69-page booklet, *Deutsche Kriegsgefangene in Feindesland, Amtliches Material, England,* published in 1919. In his report of May 1917, Schwyzer proposed the creation of a special compound in a camp in which to place crippled men, including those from Handforth POW Camp in Cheshire, under the care of the many unemployed German Red Cross men.

According to Schwyzer's 1917 report, Pattishall now had 12 satellite working camps. These were at Glendon (150 men) in Northamptonshire, Uppingham (200 men) in Rutland, Huntingdon (75 men), Linton (70 men) in Cambridgeshire, Woburn (131 men) and Southill (150 men) in Bedfordshire, Panshanger (162 men) in Hertfordshire, and further afield Buxton (200 men) and Narborough (100 men) in Norfolk, Martlesham (200 men) in Suffolk, Joyce Green (40 men) in Kent, and Lewes (115 men) in Sussex. [Corby Camp, albeit in Northamptonshire, was not under Pattishall at this time, but held 200 men.] During 1917 Pattishall took on working camps at Kidbrook and Richborough in Kent and Sompting in Sussex. These and the camps at Glendon, Joyce Green and Narborough were closed soon afterwards; Uppingham became a satellite of Brocton in Staffordshire while others were set up by the end of the year.

Letter-writing carried on apace – about 5,000 letters a week were dispatched from the Pattishall Camp and its working camps. In general the men's health was good, and the food and nutrition "about sufficient". However, "The mentality of the prisoners is of course not as good as that of men in working camps, and most of them would be much happier if they could do agricultural or forestry work." This is, no doubt, a reference to the effects of boredom and incipient depression to which POWs were exposed.

Another Swiss Legation visited Pattishall Camp on 23rd October 1917, this time Dr A L Vischer was the inspector. Grattan, now a full Colonel, was still Commandant, and Lieut Turner the Medical Officer. In this report we are provided with the names of the four Compound Leaders, *Obermaschinist* Martens, *Oberstauermann* Thamm, *Feldwebel* Scheffel and *Offizierstellvertreter* Schlesinger, yet another rare opportunity to discover the identity of some of the camp inmates. There were now 3,493 POWs in the Camp, 42 of whom were sailors while another 42 men were in the hospital. The men now received 4oz of fresh vegetables and 4oz of potatoes daily; however, in a dormitory hut for 200 men there were only five light bulbs whose power was "diminished through long use". Parcels from "Relief Agencies in Holland and Switzerland had, in many cases, arrived opened with articles missing." One of the POWs had assaulted a *Feldwebel* (Sergeant Major) and was awaiting a Court Martial, so we have the impression that all was not quite as content as on previous visits.

Further inspections of the Camp were made on 19th March 1918 and on 12th November 1918 and reports on these prepared on 25th March and 16th November by Dr A de Sturler, Special Attaché from the Swiss Legation, but so far we have been unable to locate these reports in England. That of 12th November would certainly make interesting reading if news of the Armistice on the previous day had reached Pattishall – although we should not forget that a state of war still existed between Germany and the Allies until the ratification of various peace treaties during 1919.

The final major report on activities at Pattishall Camp was composed by Dr A de Sturler and Monsieur R de Sturler of the Swiss Legation on 3rd May 1919, following their inspection on 23rd April. Col. Grattan remained as Commandant but the Medical Officer was now Capt. Rose of the RAMC. On that day there were 1,110 men in Compound I, 1,220 in Compound II, 1,100 in Compound III and 1,079 in Compound IV, a total of 4,509 POWs among whom were about 1,000 *Feldwebels* and *Unteroffiziers* (NCOs). 1,500 of the men were awaiting transfer to France, having been selected as fit for general labour there. Attached to Pattishall were now 161 satellite Working Camps, including the Agricultural Groups and Depots with a total of 14,537 POWs. Once again the names of the Compound

Leaders were recorded, but this time we are given also the German Regiments to which they belonged, i.e., *Vizefeldwebels* Bohlert (79 Inf. Regt.), Nolte (472 Inf. Regt.), Schaper (Ul. Regt. 11) and Mossinger (Pion. Regt. 25). These four men were able to speak freely but confidentially to the Swiss inspectors, expressing "a natural longing to hear that this captivity may soon come to an end". [*Vizefeldwebel* is literally a Vice Sergeant Major.]

The Camp was, "... and has been for some considerable time quite free from influenza", although in the Hospital were "about a dozen cases of Enteritis with diarrhoea [*sic*] the origin of which had not been traced with certitude". There were also several POWs with various disabilities wishing to be repatriated preferentially; however, apart from private Schmiemann, POW No. 35513, who had a paralysed left arm and had lost one eye, the inspectors could offer no promises of swift repatriation.

In the Library of Congress in Washingon DC, we have found three later items of correspondence relating to POWs held at Pattishall. These are between the Camp's Assistant Commandant Major F E Foulger and the US Postal authorities, transmitted via the American Embassy in London and the Secretary of State in Washington, but these letters are of a quite different nature. All relate to money orders sent from America in 1918 and 1919 by different parties to six of Pattishall's POWs, D Alber POW No.3063, H Bussacker POW No.32925, W Dresdner POW No.10765, W Duddeck POW No.34908, L Lorenz POW No.11743, and P Schinhofen POW No.11538; the total value of the orders was £8 8s.7d, at that time equivalent to $41.04. The correspondence is so ridiculously, and maybe typically, bureaucratic that we have chosen not to include it here.

It is perhaps fitting that we should conclude this chapter by quoting verbatim the final sentences of the final major report of May 1919:

"Pattishall fully deserves its reputation as being a well managed camp. The discipline is good and the prisoners of war are treated with great fairness and consideration".

Fig 3.1. Some of the Eastcote POWs (1916 book)

Fig 3.2. POWs in dormitory hut (1916 book)

Fig 3.3. POW bakers at work (1916 book)

Fig 3.4. Guard and bored POWs (1916 book)

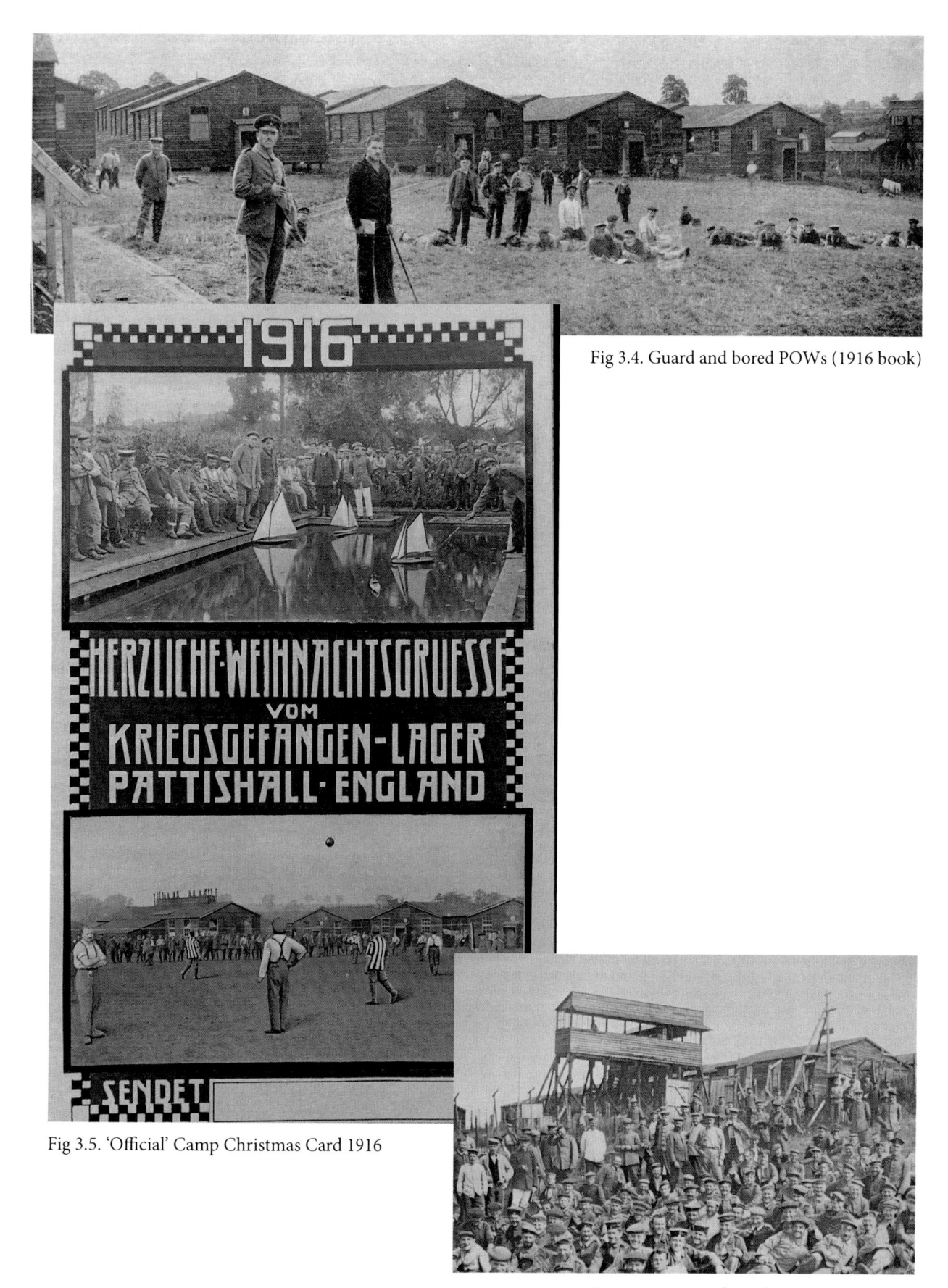

Fig 3.5. 'Official' Camp Christmas Card 1916

Fig 3.6. POWs and watch tower (1916 book)

Fig 3.7. POW Krauplatz at Pattishall (C Chapman)

Fig 3.8. Camp theatre performance (C Chapman)

Fig 3.9. Pattishall Camp guards (I Illingworth)

4. ESCAPEES

Some POWs seem to have the drive to escape in their blood; indeed, one escapee from Pattishall, when re-captured, "… regarded it as a soldier's duty, be he British or German, to escape if possible and get back to his country." [Ref.4.1]. However, escaping from a camp was one thing, escaping from Britain and reaching Germany an entirely different matter. What of these escapees, their appearance and manner? Reports of escape and re-capture in local and national newspapers sometimes offer us a name or description of features and clothing worn at the time.

Mark [Ref.4.2] names many of over 500 POWs who escaped from British Camps, including twenty-two men from Kegworth in September 1917 (the largest number from a camp in Britain). We know of eighteen men from Eastcote/Pattishall. Machray [Ref.4.3] states that nationally only four POWs got out of the country. *The Times*, the *Police Gazette* and the local press all gave space to such events because reports on escapees were features for public titillation as well as concern.

When reading accounts on escapes, one is invariably impressed by four factors – the ease of escape for some, resourcefulness of the escapees, the absence of recognition by the general public, and the considerable distance from a camp that some prisoners reached. Against this must be set the comment from one member of a delegation inspecting Eastcote Camp, that there was little incentive for prisoners to escape since they had such a comfortable time. On the other hand, boredom as much as anything could cause some prisoners to attempt a break.

The first person to escape from Eastcote Camp was Alfred Stockhurst; he got away on 28th October 1914 but made it only as far as Foster's Booth, less than a mile from the Camp, before being captured. When taken to Towcester Magistrates' Court he claimed that he wanted to join the British army and take his place on the battlefield. We have already mentioned another escapee – the unnamed seaman caught as a stoker in 1915 on a British collier supplying the Home Fleet, three months after escaping from Eastcote. He and Stockhurst were two of the eighteen men, of the thousands passing through the Camp, recorded as having escaped from Eastcote/Pattishall.

Three 'enemy aliens' who escaped in August 1915 were captured and taken, according to the *Northampton Herald* of 13th August 1915, "to a military concentration camp at Handforth"; but this could be misleading because Handforth then held only civilians and as the POWs at Eastcote were merchant seamen they may not have been taken to a military camp. The *Northampton Mercury* referred equally misleadingly to "a military internment camp near Crewe". A month later, on the night of 12th September 1915, two seamen, Wilhelm Wetzel and Hermann Yoras, escaped from Eastcote Camp. Sadly for them, they were at liberty for only a few hours, and were arrested in Northampton shortly before midnight.

No POWs were reported as escaping from Eastcote during 1916; however, in early May 1917 three military personnel, Lt. Gustav Lutz, Sgt. Major Wilhelm Landes and Corporal Walter Rivera, were able to break out and reach Wrentham near Southwold on the Suffolk coast. The *East Suffolk Gazette* for 8th May 1917 recorded their activities. The date of their escape is not given but their means lost nothing in the telling and made a hero of a local policeman.

With arc lights burning and sentries on patrol, Lutz and his colleagues got through the electric fence at Pattishall using a forked stick placed between the wires, giving them an opening through which, wearing gloves, they crawled (Fig.4.1). They took a train, sitting in a carriage full of British soldiers who regaled them with insults about the Kaiser and Germans in general. Corporal Rivera wore a civilian cap and his field-grey overcoat and service top-boots, all German issue. Arriving at Cambridge, the three left the station unchallenged and walked into the town where Lutz's fluent English enabled him to make purchases in shops whilst the others stood outside.

From Cambridge Lutz, Landes and Rivera travelled by rail to Ipswich where they again changed trains, moving freely amongst military and civilian policemen, reaching Halesworth. They then walked to Southwold arriving late on Saturday night. On Sunday they made for Wrentham on a country road. P.C. Seaman was in plain clothes when the trio came into view. The *Gazette* tells us: "The prisoners' appearance aroused his suspicions and he challenged them and discovered who they were."

The newspaper congratulated Constable Seaman for his shrewdness since he had no prior knowledge of any POW escapes in the area. Apart from a scratch on the hands of one of the prisoners, sustained when scrambling through Pattishall's barbed wire, they were all as fit as their *sang-froid*. The Suffolk local paper was alarmed that they had found it so easy to escape detection by any of the public and military personnel in whose company much of their journey took place.

The three were soon returned to Pattishall and were court marshalled on 12th May 1917. When the Camp was visited on that day by Acland and Anstruther (see above) the trio were incarcerated in the Camp's "clean, airy and sufficiently lighted" cells, "a great contrast to those in which we hear that our men are confined in Germany". Acland described the three as "bright pleasant looking lads who seemed in no way depressed". A Gustav Lutz later got away from Kegworth POW Camp with 21 others on 27th September 1917; was he the same escapee as from Pattishall? It was certainly 'our Pattishall Lutz' who declared it his duty to escape, as we quoted above.

On 31st August 1917 seven further POWs contrived an escape from Pattishall but did not get as far as the trio in May had achieved before they were re-captured. The escapees in August were Max Ball, Wilhelm Gitzen, Herman Harte, Arthur Kerst, Heinrich Muller, Wilhelm Schulte and Walter Schulz. As six of them wore German naval uniform, they would all have been combatants rather than NSFU Merchant Seamen from the original internees of 1914, particularly as we know that civilians had been moved from the Camp in July 1916. Scotland Yard published descriptions of the men:

"Max Frederick Ball, German soldier (24); complexion fresh, hair brown, eyes grey, medium build, height 5ft 5in; dress, German military uniform.
Wilhelm Gitzen, German sailor (30); complexion pale, hair brown, stout build, height 5ft 9½ins, walks with slouching gait; dress, German naval uniform.
Herman Harte (22); complexion fresh, hair sandy and close cropped, eyes blue, slight build, height, 5ft 9in; dress, German naval uniform.
Arthur Kerst (25); complexion fair, hair brown, eyes blue, slight build, height 5ft 9in. thin face, speaks English fluently; dress, German naval uniform.
Heinrich Muller (22) German sailor; complexion fresh, hair brown, eyes brown, medium build, height 5ft 5in; dress, German naval uniform, speaks English
Wilhelm Schulte (26); complexion fresh, hair brown, eyes grey, stout build, height 5ft 7in, dress, German naval uniform.
Walter Herman Schulz (21); complexion fresh, hair brown and curly, eyes grey, medium build, height 5ft 4in; dress, German naval uniform." [Ref.4.4].

"They were run to earth in a plantation between Denton and Whiston" [villages about 14 miles from Pattishall] according to a report in the *Northampton Mercury* of 7th September 1917, but not before the authorities had lost sight of them at Rothersthorpe; later sightings at Preston Deanery and Hackleton were not reported to the police. Now enter local labourers Tompkins and Burgh, the latter carrying a gun and told by the former he had seen the prisoners. Burgh "found the men sleeping peacefully...having taken shocks of corn from a neighbouring field....as beds..., [took] their boots off and made themselves comfortable..."

P.C. Shortland of Brafield on the Green and P.C. Redley of Northampton, who had been alerted, aroused the escapees whereupon "They put up their hands and surrendered just as though they had been on the field of battle". The report continued:
"They were in a very bedraggled condition after their two days and a night in the open and were doubtless glad to be caught.... The reason they gave for trying to escape was that they were tired of being in camp and that they wanted to do some work. Some of the men have been prisoners for over three years. They were all wearing the clothing in which they left the camp....it was thought the men were making for Peterborough with the view, if possible, of getting to the East Coast."
It is conceivable that this was the route taken in 1915 by the un-named seaman who ended up as a stoker on a collier before being apprehended.

The last person to escape from Pattishall was Heinrich Schultz, on 4/5th August 1919. He was recaptured on 11th August near Wolverton, about 15 miles away in Buckinghamshire. According to the *Northampton Mercury* of 15th August:
"...P.C.Chilver got him as he was crossing Haversham bridge, just north of Wolverton. Schultz was taken to Stony Stratford Police Station and there handed over to a military court. In his possession were articles which had been stolen from a house at Castlethorpe and a platelayer's hut near that village".

There were also prisoners who escaped from the Pattishall satellite camps such as Southill Working Camp, Old Warden, Bedfordshire in 1917: "Otto Gruhlen, age 25, height 5ft 6in, hair and moustache fair, grey eyes, medium build; dress brown cord government clothing"; he disappeared while engaged with a party of German soldiers cutting up fallen trees, but was eventually recaptured on 23rd June, a few weeks after he had absconded. In August 1918, Henrick Schmidt (25) and Theodore Jaskutla (22) escaped from Rothwell Working Camp near Kettering. A local lad, 17 year-old Thomas Gibson, who had been out rabbit shooting, saw them as he was returning home, accosted them with his double-barrelled gun and marched them to a nearby village police station. Altogether, around some 70 POWs escaped from Pattishall's satellite camps. All of these escapes, some not noted by Mark, have been thoroughly researched by Chapman – see Bibliography.

The people in whose midst the POWs were held recalled their presence with general acceptance and in some cases affection for those who, under escort, helped out on local farms or in the local quarry. Frederick Horner for instance, a Pattishall POW, became so friendly with William Nightingale's family in Eastcote when he was working nearby that he kept in touch after the war and sent photographs (Figs.4.2, 4.3) and other mementos.

Arthur Howe from Pattishall recalled in 1979 that many of the prisoners were very talented and took part in concerts and shows. They made toys and souvenirs, some of which were given to and are retained by village parishioners. A fine memento is a three-masted barque, the *Bertha* (Fig.4.4) allegedly made by some Baltic seamen, and donated to the grandparents of John Coy of Eastcote.

Punishments awarded to re-captured escapees seem to have been very much at the discretion of a military Court Martial, though were normally of up to six-months' imprisonment in a civilian gaol far away from the original POW camp. Naturally there were guidelines from relevant government departments, based on the Geneva and Hague Conventions; for example, collective punishment when a POW escaped was forbidden. We have not yet found precisely how returned escapees at Pattishall were treated, but we can see from reports of British POWs returning from Germany that at some camps 'over there' punishment was severe, and perchance in Britain the Conventions were not followed to the letter. Internationally, discussion between the German and British authorities, both directly and through intermediaries, had moved slowly from around 1917 towards agreed improved procedures in this matter. Set periods and terms of punishment were laid down. It was mid-August 1918 when new agreements were reached, but by then it was too late for most prisoners. They had only the consolation of knowing that in future conflicts belligerent nations had more appropriate rules to follow when dealing with POWs.

Fig 4.1. Eastcote Camp, general view (1916 book)

Fig 4.2. POW Horner, repatriated to Germany (A Nightingale)

Fig 4.3. Reverse of Fig 4.2. (from Horner to William Nightingale)

Fig 4.4. The Bertha (J Coy & G Perrett)

5. PRISONERS' LIVES & LETTERS

For many combatant personnel, from capture in Europe to POW Camp in Britain was a deeply unsettling and traumatic affair. Transportation, field work under fire, barbed wire prison cages open to the elements, hostility from civilians during transfer through France, across the Channel and to camps on British soil were common experiences for thousands of POWs. Accordingly, arrival at a permanent camp in Britain was the start of a more settled and in many cases less unpleasant experience. Of course, the original merchant seamen internees at Eastcote Camp suffered none of these traumas but in time, as we have already pointed out, boredom could set in for any prisoner. From 1916, when some men were transferred to working camps 'beyond the wire', we know they were happy to be away from Pattishall which they found dull with little to do. In the words of Paul Cohen-Portheim, a German civilian interned initially at Knockaloe but then, at his own request, transferred to the officers' camp at Lofthouse Park, Wakefield "time here really had to be killed for it was the arch-enemy" [Ref.5.1]. For others, things were even worse for as the war dragged on the mental disorientation that we mentioned in Chapter 1 developed into depression, melancholia and neurasthenia, which became termed 'barbed-wire disease'.

Of the POW Camps throughout the British Isles and the fortunes of their inmates in general, the comments of August Gallinger, looking back in 1922, are noteworthy: "Naturally, there was much to find fault with [in the British Camps], but it was generally due to lack of organization, not to hatred, and except for isolated cases, was not caused by brutality or the desire to vent one's spleen on individuals who were in no way responsible for the war." [Ref.5.2]. From what we have discovered about Eastcote/Pattishall Camp, its management was somewhat better than Gallinger had experienced, but in the remainder of this chapter let us divulge some of our discoveries.

The military authorities published Camp Rules and from these we can deduce what life, at least in theory, could be like for those 'behind the wire' at Pattishall. It is important for us to bear in mind that under the military regimes, POWs were encouraged to participate and play key roles in the running of the camps with their own management and committee structures. Detail on camp life and conditions were seldom the subject of prisoners' letters because of censorship, but even so, we can glean some fascinating snippets here and there from their correspondence.

One of the first letters that we have seen from Eastcote Camp was written on 6th November 1914, well before the NFSU handed over the Camp management to the military authorities. Alfred Brunner, allocated POW No.1390, used the Camp's own NSFU headed notepaper to contact Maria Urbaučich (apparently his girlfriend from the endearing terms he used) in Trieste, then in Austria-Hungary. He explained that he had been detained in Liverpool attempting to return to Germany to fight for the Kaiser and his homeland but the British authorities had prevented him doing so and had sent him to Eastcote. It is significant to note that while the envelope in which he put his letter was a standard issue bearing the 'Prisoners of War' imprint and 'No Stamp Required', at this period Brunner, in common with other detainees, was permitted to use NSFU notepaper.

When Ernst Clauberg, identified as POW No.2079, wrote from Company 67 in Compound IV at Eastcote on 12th May 1916 to the August family in Solingen, his letter was censored. He wrote on a plain sheet of paper and enclosed it in a plain envelope (Fig.5.1). Clauberg tells his friends that he is cheerful, Eastcote is in a beautiful area, and although it is summer, it is raining – [so we can observe no change in English weather over the past century]. Significantly he found that time passed very quickly, so the boredom experienced by others had not hit him, at least not yet.

After the civilian internees had been removed from Eastcote in July 1916, leaving only combatant POWs, arrangements became more regulated. Upon arrival at the Camp each prisoner went through a common processing procedure. He had to complete a standard form, the first part of which was filled up by the Commandant, the second either by the prisoner himself or at his dictation by a clerk. The completed form was sent to the POWIB in London. Camp rules were conveyed (in German) to the POWs from the Commandant, probably through the 'captain' of the Company to which they were posted. Based on rules drawn up by the War Office Lt Col Ansley issued those for Eastcote Camp, which we outline here in translation:

"…this camp's prisoners are grouped into sections. Each section consists of the occupants of one quarter of a hut. The members of a section must select a 'hut senior' whose duty it is to support the Commandant in maintaining order and discipline."

Company heads/captains were responsible to the Commandant for the behaviour of their fellow POWs. The captains also chose camp 'police officers' who acted on their behalf and whose instructions the POWs were bound to obey. It is clear that Ansley intended, as did his superiors, that the Camp's internal management was the responsibility of its inmates. We should remember that all POWs were subject to Military Law and that the rules applied to both combatants and non-combatants - the latter could have found this arrangement considerably less attractive than the regime previously established by Wilson and the NSFU.

"As regards wilful insubordination or resistance against officers, guards or sentinels or other acts of insurgency, weapons will be used if necessary". Whilst we have no record of any prisoner at Pattishall being shot, there were cases in other POW Camps in Britain, including a riot at Douglas Camp on the Isle of Man in November 1914 when four prisoners were shot and nineteen injured, and shootings by guards at Leigh Camp in 1915, and at Oswestry and Dorchester Camps in 1919.

There was much sense in Ansley's requirement that "Since guards do not speak German and prisoners of war may not understand English, the company heads must explain the command stop".

The Camp had two parallel barbed wire perimeter fences, with an area between them called the neutral zone, entry to which was forbidden at night, and only with a sentry's permission in the daytime – to retrieve a ball for instance. Conversation with other than fellow POWs was allowed only with the Commandant's permission.

Alcoholic drinks and gambling were strictly forbidden. Reveille was at 6.30am; breakfast 7.45 to 8.30; lunch 12 noon to 1pm and dinner 5pm to 6pm. From 9.30pm all prisoners had to remain in their huts with 'Lights off' at 10 pm and silence everywhere. There were 'review' parades at least twice a day, presumably to check numbers etc. Cooks, one from each hut, began their work at 5am. The huts were to be tidied on Mondays and Thursdays and in good weather bedding was to be aired daily. Each hut was to provide working crews when required, in turns.

Each POW was allowed to write two letters a week using only the paper and ink provided and in Latin letters on the lines on the sheet. Visits were permitted once a month in the interpreter's office for one hour only on a Monday and Tuesday. There was access to newspapers subject to the Commandant's approval, paid for in advance and booked through each 'hut senior'. This privilege was subject to one proviso:

"The approval will be revoked if demonstrations are staged as a result of newspaper articles."

The usual punishment for anyone who broke the Camp Rules was the withdrawal of the right to send or receive correspondence. This appears to have been a universally accepted means of dealing with indiscipline, apart from incarceration in a camp's own prison cells. Re-captured escapees were subject to Courts Martial as explained in the previous chapter.

From time to time complaints were taken beyond the Commandant's remit to higher authority. For instance, in July 1917 the Swiss Legation in London received a *note verbale* from Berlin:

"A prisoner of war interned at Pattishall Camp, Towcester, has complained in a letter addressed to his relatives, that the prisoners in this camp are told, in order to torment them, that on their return to Germany they could be exposed to general neglect, excluded from all promotion, and deprived of the privileges formerly received; through the circulation of this report a great disquietude has been excited among the prisoners. The Foreign Office requests the Swiss Legation to mention the complaint to the British Government...and to devote its attention to the matter on visiting the above-mentioned camp."

This matter was also relayed on the same day to the Royal Netherlands Legation. On 9th August the Swiss duly sent a letter to the Foreign Office: "....that men interned there [Pattishall Camp] are told that on their return to Germany they will be subjected to universal contempt...". The Swiss offered to transmit any reply the Foreign Office cared to make. On 18th August the following duly appeared:

" Enquiry shows that no prisoner of war in this, or it may be said in any other camp, has ever been told by any officer or other member of the camp staff that he would be exposed to penalties of any kind on his return to Germany. Any report on the subject which has reached the German authorities is probably due to the idea existing among the German NCOs that punishment will be meted out to them on their return to their native country should they volunteer for work. In one case a German NCO who had so volunteered, refused to sign a receipt for his pay on the grounds that if it came to the knowledge of his Government that he had so worked, the family allowances in Germany would be stopped. The wife of a German NCO in this camp when writing to her husband told him that her allowance had been stopped as he had received pay for working in England."

There the matter rests for we have found no further information.

By chance, on the desks of both of us stand small earthenware inkpots (Fig.5.2), each with a cork shrunken with age. Ninety-five years ago men dipped their nibs into ink held in pots like these which, as we know from the Camp Rules, was the only ink permitted. Officialdom had strict rules about ink and secrecy. How many POWs used one of these pots which we recovered from the remnants of Pattishall Camp, we shall never know. What we do know, without any doubt at all, is that letters were as important for POWs and their families as they were for combatants at the front.

All correspondence to and from Eastcote/Pattishall and its satellites was censored throughout the war. To simplify and speed the process, letter sheets replacing envelopes were introduced in mid-1916. They were of glazed paper to prevent secret inks being used with 23 printed lines for the message and closed with a tuck-in flap or tongue. They were inspected and in London a numbered censor's label affixed, but not sealing the flap if destined for Germany - thereby enabling German censors to examine letters without damaging them. By August 1918 a new design of letter sheet, Patent No.2333/15, was introduced, available in two styles with straight or diagonal cuts at the folds to facilitate a slip-in closure, although many letters from Pattishall continued to be written on the flap style sheet until at least July 1919. During most of the war POWs were restricted to sending two letters a week, though from around September 1919 this was unofficially relaxed by camp commandants. There was no limit on letters received and all incoming parcels were opened by camp officials in the presence of the prisoner. After the Third Battle of Ypres on 31st July 1917, some 5,000 German POWs were sent to England and the volume of mail increased rapidly towards the end of the year and into 1918; furthermore, after the Armistice the volume of letters increased exponentially, resulting in a total of over 21.5 million items of incoming and outgoing POW mail in 1918, compared with 13.25 million in 1917 [Ref.5.3].

Copies of the picture postcard that we described in Chapter 3, produced for POWs to send at Christmas 1916, were simply rubber-stamped 'P.C.' (a censor's mark – though there were several styles for this cypher) before being dispatched. We have no notion of how many of these cards were sent, but we know that prisoners Böhm, POW No.3135, Büttel POW No.3142, and Dauber, POW No.6580, all in Compound I and Company 6, addressed copies of the card to their friends and families but added no messages to the German greetings printed on the front.

The very nature of the prescribed format of the page on which the POWs were obliged to write from 1916, the presence of censors who scrutinised the letters, and the structure and daily routine of the camps in which they were incarcerated, meant there was little scope for variety and real news in their correspondence. However, let us take a peep at some more of the correspondence that we have read from and to men held at Pattishall. All letters were in German, some in the old-style [hard to decipher] handwriting; we offer translations here.

Joseph Schmidt, POW No. 23146, sent some photographs to his parents at Steinach in Germany along with nearly fifty letters. In one photograph some forty men are standing, sitting and kneeling against a wooded backdrop (Fig.5.3). In another, thirty of them are taking a break from work, probably at the Descote limestone quarry near Dalscote, about half a mile from Eastcote (Fig.5.4). In each photograph they wear German issue uniforms and caps, their resigned looks reflecting the same sentiment as shown in their letters.

In one of the surviving letters, Schmidt wrote to his mother and sister on 22nd September 1918 telling them he had received two parcels and two letters. None of the parcels sent so far had been lost. He asks them not to send any more beans since he cannot cook them. In a postscript he sends greetings to Marie, to the well-known Steinacher and to 'big' Wendel. Another letter, nearly a year later is dated 29th July 1919: he had received two letters from them on 27th July dated 5th and 20th May. The news of contemporary life in Germany angered him in that the authorities appeared to be pre-occupied with domestic politics and to have forgotten all about the POWs. He asked his family not to write so much on this in future and advised:
"when the red Joseph [Communist party] comes again do not give them anything because it is only for them. This is the mood in our prison camp."

Here is a clue that the state of post-war Germany was a worry to the POWs in Britain and it shows in letters such as this.

In 1968, Günter Schmidt, grandson of Joseph and Frau Schmidt, visited Pattishall seeking the Camp where his grandfather had been held. Like his father and grandfather Günter became a forester near Steinach - so the prisoner in a forestry working camp of 1918 comes full circle with the grandson. Austin Nightingale gave Günter hospitality and showed him round the site of the former Camp. They kept up correspondence for a few years and in one letter Günter wrote:

"When I told my story [of a visit to England] to my parents and grandmother they were thrilled. I think my grandfather would have jumped for joy hearing of my adventures. When my grandmother was putting her things in good order [in 1988], she found some photographs of my grandfather taken when he was prisoner of war in England."

After much searching in Germany we were able in 2012 to locate Günter Schmidt once more and he has now shared with us further experiences of his grandfather as a POW at Pattishall.

Many prisoners valued gifts sent by neutral benefactors in Switzerland, individuals, the ICRC and other welfare organisations. The POWIB ensured free postage in accordance with the Hague Convention. Infantryman Joseph Wiezel, POW No.3999 of Company 9 in Compound I, received food and money from Zimmerlin, Forcart & Company in Basel. In mid-September 1917, Emil Kiefer, POW No. 5370, wrote to the Bureau for POWs in Switzerland, trying to find out who had sent him a parcel. The Bureau seemingly informed him that the donors were the same as had helped Wiezel, namely Zimmerlin & Co of Basel, as on 28th October he wrote from Pattishall's working camp at Rothwell, Northamptonshire thanking them. In June and November 1918 Emil Karle, POW No.18701, based in hut 1440, although away at a working camp when he wrote in June, sent letters to Councillor Phillipp in Basel thanking him for two gifts of money.

The letter writers often grumbled at the infrequency of mail which only added to their anxieties. Wilhelm Kornith, POW No. 15022, of Company 62 in Compound IV, wrote to his mother, Emilie and his sisters Gretel and Wildrut in Berlin on 18th January 1918. When he wrote again on 8th April he bewailed the shortage of letters and parcels. He had last heard from Augusta on 5th March, though she had sent 25 Marks and intended sending 10 Marks weekly, but nothing had come of it, as with parcels - a rather different scenario from the deliveries promised from the camp authorities though, of course, the parcels could have been 'mislaid' *en route* in Germany, in Britain, or anywhere in between. Misdelivery was not impossible, though we should not forget that there were also acute shortages of food and other goods in both countries resulting from naval blockades.

Friedrich Neuberger, POW No.15155, known to his friends as Fritz, took a cheerful view of the nineteen months he had been at Pattishall, living in Hut 220; on 7th January 1919, in the fifteenth letter he had written to his friend Max Jahn in Reuss ältere Linie, he pens:

"My Dear Good Friend! Today I can write 3 nineteens, because now I have been an English captive for nineteen months at nine o'clock in the morning and this [year] happens to be 1919….Things aren't really too bad, I am still fit and well. I hope this year will be better than last year, which brought me sadness three times. When these few lines arrive home, I shall perhaps not be far from home, because that's how things are looking….."

A POW we know a little more about is Karl Wiedemann, POW No.18666, who was based in hut 1410 from at least May 1918 until August 1919. He wrote letters to his wife Anna and his children Karl and Gertrude in Linden, a suburb of Hannover. On 21st May 1918 he asked them to send him a sewing kit, some tobacco and a pipe. In Wiedemann's case both his metal identity disc (*Erkennungsmarke*) and service record have survived (Fig.5.5), so we know he was born on 3rd September 1874 and captured at Ribecourt on 20th November 1917 by Scottish infantrymen. From Wiedemann's letters we can see that by 15th August 1919 he had been transferred to one of Pattishall's working camps at Maldon, Essex.

The metal identity disc of another prisoner, Richard Salbenblatt, born on 11th April 1896, and from Bechtshüttel in Gifhorn District of Lower Saxony, was unearthed somewhat corroded (Fig.5.6) on the Camp ground many years after he had been repatriated. This artefact alone – we have no letters – tells us that he was among the POWs held at Pattishall some time between 1914 and 1919.

Joseph Müller, POW No. 5376 sent a photograph to fellow prisoner, Julius Bölle, POW No. 3123, presumably of themselves and friends: they may well be the ones seated at the front whilst their colleagues stand behind [Ref.5.4]. Some are holding cigars and pipes. The soldier second right wears a Kaiser Wilhelm moustache. In the background two other POWs lie on the grass beneath the trees and beyond them is Hut 101. Photographs give an immediacy and identity to the letters; here are their subjects looking out at us and, in the case of two of them, no longer just names.

We know of at least two members of German U-boat crews held at Pattishall in 1918 and 1919. On 12th May 1918 the 46,000 ton *RMS Olympic* [sister ship to the *Titanic*], carrying American troops to France, spotted *U-103* on the surface about 45 miles south of Falmouth.

The *Olympic* rammed and sunk the submarine. Engine Room Petty Officer Paul Wadewitz was one of the thirty-one survivors picked up by an American escort vessel. He became POW No.21773 when he joined the other prisoners in Pattishall Camp. Wadewitz wrote many letters from Pattishall - by March 1919 he was on his fifty-seventh. In his seventy-eighth letter on 27th May 1919 he thanked his mother for three parcels that had arrived on 27th April, asked if the strike by the road and rail workers in Hamburg was over, and told her the weather in Pattishall was beautiful every day. When his father wrote to him in September 1919, censorship of POW letters, as with all mail from late 1918, had ceased. Second Petty Officer Max Caplan, POW No.26207, from U-boat *UB-124*, sunk on 20th July 1918, was more sanguine. When writing to his sisters in Cöpenick, near Berlin on 26th December 1918, thanking them for their letters, he told them he did nothing on Christmas Day, apart from noting the date on the calendar; he asked them to thank his fiancée for her letters and added there was "nothing new for me, always sorrow and monotony".

POW Bruno Albrecht was an even more prolific correspondent than Wadewitz penning at least 102 letters between 1918 and 1919 to Frau Margarete Albrecht, his beloved Grete in Berlin. We have access to twenty of these letters from the second one that he wrote on 28th October 1918 from Blackdown Camp (nearby, or maybe synonymous with, Frith Hill) to the one hundred and second that he wrote on 11th October 1919 from Pattishall, to where he had been transferred in late 1918 or early 1919. By October 1919 he had received in return eighty-three letters from Grete (Fig.5.7). While at Blackdown he had been allocated POW No.4912, but on arrival at Pattishall was given, as was normal practice, a new identity, POW No.34480. Although Albrecht was in Compound II for all of his time at Pattishall he was initially in Company 29 and then from July 1919 in Company 26.

Walter Becker, POW No.32878 of Company 13 in Compound I, received a sentimental picture postcard from his dearest Hannchen in Berlin to celebrate the New Year in early 1919. She had received a letter from him on 12th December 1918 and used the festive season to remind him of their mutual affection.

The letters of Fritz Berwig POW No 16574, initially in Company 34, then in Company 28, and from mid February 1918 sleeping in hut 290 in Compound II at Pattishall Camp, illustrate the concerns of prisoner and spouse between January 1918 and his last letter of 24th August 1919. Berwig addresses his letters to his wife, Maria living near Kempten, Bavaria.

He had been taken prisoner in June 1917 shortly before the 3rd Battle of Ypres. Initially his letters were full of optimism referring to friends and relations. On 17th January 1918 he wrote:

"My very darling wife, here is another letter to you, my joy above mountains and sea. I am well as I hope you and our scampish son are. Please tell Head Teacher Frey that I send best wishes to his son Carl and that I am better. I hope to receive a letter from you soon. I do so long for one. Please call my family and give them my love and tell them my new address. The post seems to be getting through faster than it did. Don't worry about me. Give my love to your family too, especially Georgie. I do so hope that your letter and the jacket will get here soon. I send you love and kisses from your loving Fritz…Give my love to the Böhm family. See you soon."

A month later such optimism was ebbing and many of his later letters are full of himself, his homesickness, and only once, on 19th June 1918, does he refer to work:

"Here I do farm-work. Most recently I have been making hay, but it's all done quite differently from the way we do it at home [near Kempten]…we are taken to the farmer early in the mornings by the guards; we work under constant supervision and then in the evening we are taken back to camp, and so it goes on day after day until peace is declared".

Such changes of mood could have been the effects of settling in, enforced idleness or the longing to get home. It is well to appreciate that Fritz Berwig had lived through a serious influenza epidemic in which over twenty POWs in the Pattishall Camp had died. He was not alone in feeling this desperation; his wife also shared it, feeling utterly hopeless. He was disturbed by some news from Maria raising doubts in his mind about her fidelity – but invariably he comes back to their love for each other and their son.

POW No.19935, Musketier Albert Krental of Hut 540, was a prisoner about whom we have more information thanks to his grandson Wolfgang Paland. Krental's service record book shows he was born on 21st July 1895 in Salzgitter, Hannover, where his father was the postman. His family was large - two sisters, Minna and Grete and four brothers, Karl, Heinrich, Wilhelm and Walter. All brothers, except Walter, served in the war. Until 1914 Albert was a bespoke-shoemaker but a shortage of leather and customers forced him to switch jobs to the post office. On 10th May 1916 he joined as a Reserve Recruit and was posted to the Rekruten Depot, Erstatz Batallion in a Prussian regiment.

On 21st July Krental arrived at the IX Army Corps Recruits' Depot where he was pushed through musketry training, in which he did well, and was then drafted as a musketier to the

163rd Schleswig-Holstein Infantry Regiment. Between 15th October 1916 and 30th March 1917 he saw action at Loos and Ypres during which time he was awarded the Iron Cross II Class for his service on the Somme (Fig.5.8). On 1st April 1917 he was posted to the Arras sector and was in the front line at Neuville-Vitasse when his detachment's position was overrun by the London Scottish Regiment on 9th April. The War Diaries of the 163rd Infantry Regiment record that: "at 07.00 hours the 2nd Company occupied K2 [Telegraph Hill] Trench… Leutnant D.R.Kesler ordered his men to make clear for action…about 07.30 hours 2nd Company started to fire with rifle and machine guns against the assaulting Englishmen."

Krental recalled: "I could see only a little…the English were 400m away. It was misty… Carl Moll, next to me, suddenly fell down groaning. I saw his head was smashed perhaps by a shell splinter…He died later in a British hospital." From later reports we can discover that the London Scottish soldiers came in partly to the rear of Albert's position which he described as "hidden in the earth of Neuville-Vitasse [where] I survived the day without a scratch, whereas my comrades died around me."

After being captured by the British, Krental spent several months in France before being transferred to Pattishall in October 1917. He remained there, with occasional and much-welcomed breaks at satellite working-camps in Suffolk, until September 1919. Then he was shipped via France on the *Oratava* (Fig.5.9) to Wilhelmshaven naval base. After a celebration dinner there, he returned to his parents' home in Salzgitter on October 8th 1919. Initially, Krental found it hard to obtain work. Eventually after working as a miner and marrying in 1921, he secured a job with the post office in Salzgitter rising to a prominent management position. He died in 1982, aged 87. In the meantime his eldest daughter Elizabeth had married and had a son, Wolfgang Paland, our correspondent.

Krental's letters, like those of his fellow-prisoners, made little reference to Pattishall Camp and the conditions there. Apart from complaining about the mail and parcel service his major concern was his family at home. On 23rd May 1918 he asked after his brothers – Heinrich serving in as a Lance Corporal in a Marine Corps, Wilhelm married to Hermione in Berlin who had been on sick leave, and his friend, Karl Friche. He wrote again on 11th August seeking news, but was unaware that his brother Karl, a medical corporal in the 10th Jager Batalllion, had been killed in the Second Battle of the Marne on 15th July 1918.

A later letter of his in August 1918 contained a photograph (Fig.5.10) of himself as a young musketier on which he had scribbled "Greetings from Mendlesham" – a considerable distance from the Orfordness working camp in Suffolk to where he had been posted. He was wearing German-issue cap and jacket with British-issue cavalry trousers and infantry puttees. He wrote that he enjoyed doing voluntary work on the land and being praised for it. He and a comrade seemed to have had a good relationship with the farmer and his children.

On 11th November 1918 the Armistice was declared. Of Krental's reaction we have no record. However, at Douglas Isle of Man Camp one of the guards recalled:
"Anyone would have thought the Germans had won…the prisoners were shouting and cheering and ecstatic with joy."

Food parcels from Grete and his parents continued to arrive from time to time. On 22nd February 1919 Krental thanked Grete for her letters of 13th December 1918 and 13th January 1919 and asked for soup cubes. He wrote again on 27th February from Orfordness, thanking his family for "sugar and rusks", hoping to be home for Easter, but was unhappy about the news coming out of Germany. When he wrote on 19th May 1919, now back at Pattishall, the conditions at home worried him so much that he begged his folk to keep their food and not send it to him for he was well fed. Like others he longed for the end of the war.

Krental's fellow-prisoner Herman Schroeder, POW No.31131 recorded his feelings of the signing of the Peace Treaty at Versailles in June 1919, news of which they had all been awaiting. Schroeder had been wounded in August 1918, captured, and cared for initially at Belmont Hospital, Surrey. He wrote to his family from there on 28th August using pencil, permitted for POWs in hospital or at working camps - in parent camps only ink was allowed. By at least 27th November 1918 he had been moved to Pattishall when he again wrote home. He sent further letters on 9th May, 1st July, and 8th and 13th September 1919. In his July letter, we can see that he had a grasp of the realities of his family's situation:

"Pattishall, Tuesday 1 July 1919:

Dear Parents,
 At last the long-awaited peace has arrived – on Saturday 28th June at 3.12 in the afternoon, world peace was signed at Versailles by all the representatives of the Allies and Central Powers. That very evening we became aware of the signing of the Peace Treaty and in the morning of the 29th we were all eager to see what news would be brought by the English newspapers published here concerning the prisoners of war.

For us things will not be going so quickly yet; firstly the matter of the exchange must be first settled, secondly we are the conquered ones and we must wait for our time to come. The Peace Treaty will be given its validity only if four of the High Allied Powers guarantee the full validity of the Treaty, as *The Times* stated 'yesterday, all German Free States should give their signature to the signing of peace'."

Schroeder's concerns, like those of Berwig, were real enough. Repatriation had been a major problem for both Germany and Britain since the outbreak of the war. In August 1914 civilians beyond military age and women were encouraged back to their own countries. After the sinking of the *Lusitania* in May 1915, Britain ceased repatriation abruptly and interned all German males of military age, eventually most of them on the Isle of Man.

Red Cross personnel should have been repatriated throughout the war, but both sides dragged their feet on this. Many POWs at Pattishall, as we can see from their letters, believed that as a result of the Armistice on 11th November 1918, they would soon be repatriated. But initially Germany refused to accept defeat. Nevertheless, on 21st November 1918, as the first ship-loads of British POWs were sailing home, the huge German High Seas Fleet surrendered and was, in effect, interned at sea at Scapa Flow. Scores of German submarine crews surrendered soon after and they were brought ashore and interned in POW camps in Britain.

Peace talks plodded on over Christmas 1918 and all through the Spring of 1919, thus many POWs remained at Pattishall and other camps, much to their frustration – again displayed in their letters. By Summer 1919 the fear of hostilities breaking out again was very real, with the possibility that the (German) warships at Scapa Flow would be used by the Royal Navy against Germany. Although the Treaty of Versailles was signed on 18th June 1919, which required repatriation to be advanced by both sides, Germany remained unhappy with its terms. Hence on 21st June the German Admiral, Ludwig von Reuter, ordered his interned fleet at Scapa Flow to be scuppered. Chaos ensued but one outcome was many more Germans being interned in POW camps in Britain, so prolonging the process of repatriation. Added to this was the low availability of German shipping in which POWs could be taken home, and the huge numbers of mines abandoned by both sides in the English Channel making navigation difficult. The peace negotiations continued at a protracted conference in Paris, with many German POWs still unrepatriated on 10th January

1920, when the peace treaty was formally ratified, although we know that Pattishall Camp itself, even if not all its dependent camps, had been cleared of POWs by then.

Sadly, not all of Krental's and Schroeder's fellow prisoners could be repatriated. We have identified these men on page 57. Two were German NSFU members, merchant seamen at Eastcote and alien civilian internees from August 1914, Karl Möller aged 64, who died on 5th August 1915 and Emil Gumpert aged 48, who died on 28th January 1916; both were buried in Pattishall consecrated soil. On 16th February 1917 Georg Blum aged 40 died of an embolism: being a Roman Catholic his burial service on 21st February was taken by the Camp Commandant because Gibson, the Anglican vicar of Pattishall's parish church, was unwilling to do so. Seven other Catholic POWs who subsequently died while in the Camp were similarly buried at services conducted by the Commandant.

In 1918 a mutant strain of the influenza virus caused a global pandemic. The Spanish 'flu', as it was called, killed the young and the fit more readily than the frail and elderly - the normal casualties of lung infections. In two years - 1918 and 1919 - between twice and four times as many people died of this influenza as had perished in the war. Official estimates give 21 millions in Britain and globally it could have been twice that number. For combatants it began in the Spring of 1918 when soldiers in the trenches complained of sore throat, headache and loss of appetite. By Autumn the symptoms were much more severe and infection spread globally. 228,000 British people died of the disease in 1918. More than 400,000 German civilians died in the summer of 1918 in Germany. In 1920 the Ministry of Health official report stated that: "we have just passed through one of the greatest sicknesses in history, a plague which within a few months has destroyed more lives than were sacrificed in four years of a destructive war." [Ref.5.5]. It took the edge off celebrations and easy optimism.

At Pattishall Camp in 1918 there were seven POW deaths in November and two in December out of a total of eleven for all parishioners that year. In November alone six funerals were conducted in ten days, all of them after 11th November. One wonders how far these men had been already weakened by their experiences on the Western Front before they became POWs. In March and April 1919 there were six POW deaths out of thirteen in total within the whole of Pattishall parish – see page 57. During that year six of the men who died at the Camp were aged 25 and under. Men like Max Pellander (20), Otto Lesk (21),

Ludwig Sandtner (23) and August Toepelt (23) could have been called up for military service only in 1916. Clearly the crowded conditions in the Camp assisted the virus along its destructive path, accounting for half of the deaths of POWs entered in Pattishall's parish register for 1919. Strangely, the burial of Fritz Kuhle, one of the men from the Camp who died in 1919, was not recorded in the parish register, even though his death was registered with the local Registrar in Towcester and his grave in Pattishall's churchyard was clearly documented in the 1960s. In the compounds which had held tens of thousands POWs, thirty-two died during the life of the Camp, twenty-four of these in the final two years.

All of Pattishall's surviving POWs had left by early November 1919, taking with them their individual possessions, memories and experiences, some of which we have shared with you in the above pages. Eastcote House and its surrounding land, crammed with the numerous buildings and facilities that had been purpose-built over the previous five years, must have looked like a ghost town.

A few military personnel remained, but clearly insufficient to dissuade persons unknown from gaining access to one of the huts sometime in 1919 between 11th and 16th November. Helping themselves to twenty-two blankets and some POW clothing, altogether worth £11 3s, the thieves stuffed the items into sacks, and gave them to local labourer, Arthur Starmer. He carted them away on a trolley that belonged to Frederick Watts of Towcester and sold the booty to him for £5 10s. Unfortunately for Watts it had been snowing and when he collected the trolley and sacks from Starmer, his tracks were followed. The local police caught up with Starmer and Watts; then Regimental Quartermaster Sergeant Copeman of the 1st Cambridgeshire Regiment, who was stationed at the Camp, identified the contents of the sacks and confirmed the items had not been sold, so Starmer and Watts ended up on 21st November before the Towcester magistrates, one of whom was William George Stops. On 28th November Starmer's case was dismissed but Watts was fined £10 for receiving stolen goods. Only five years before, William George Stops had Chaired a Rural District Council Meeting that, as we saw in Chapter 2, had queried the very existence of Eastcote Camp, Pattishall. Could this be termed 'exoneration'?

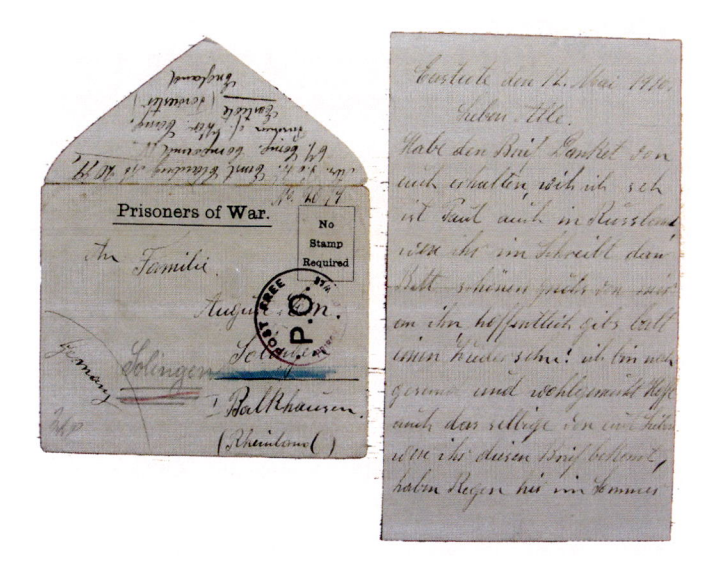

Fig 5.1. POW Clauberg's letter (C Chapman)

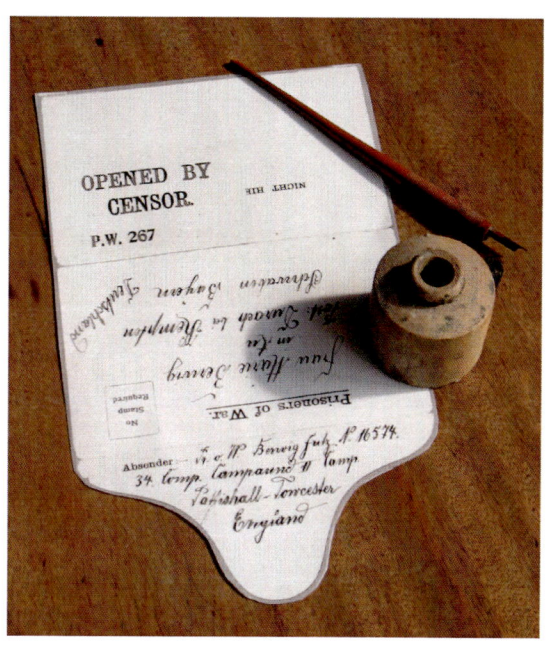

Fig 5.2. Inkpot from Pattishall Camp (R Moss)

Fig 5.3. POW Schmidt and fellow POWs at Pattishall (G Schmidt)

Fig 5.4. POW Schmidt and fellow POWs at Descote Quarry (G Schmidt)

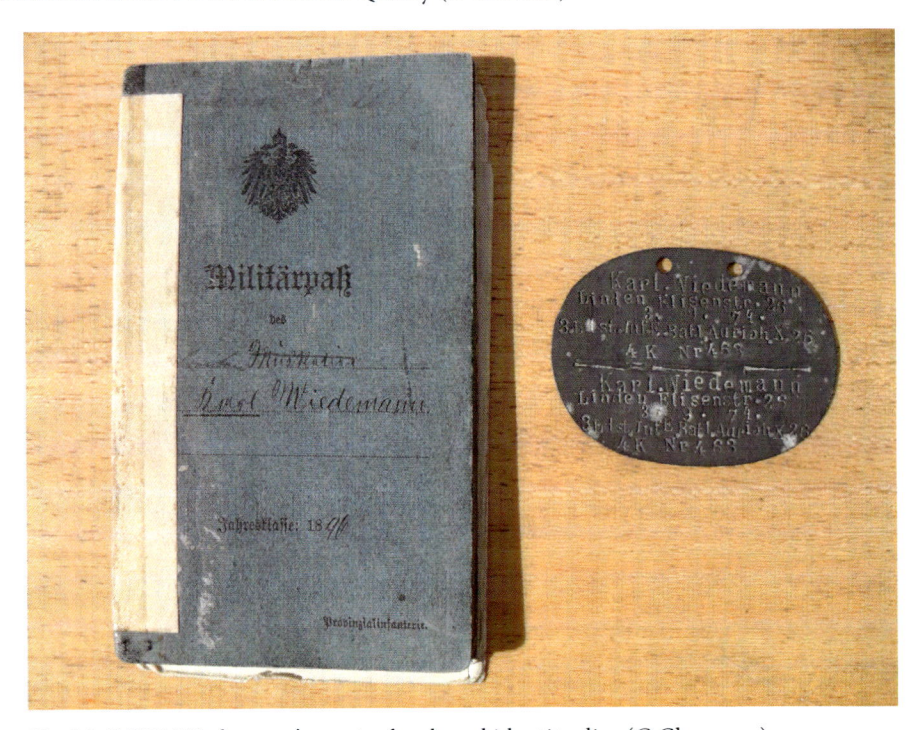

Fig 5.5. POW Wiedemann's service book and identity disc (C Chapman)

Fig 5.6. POW Salbenblatt's identity disc (A Nightingale)

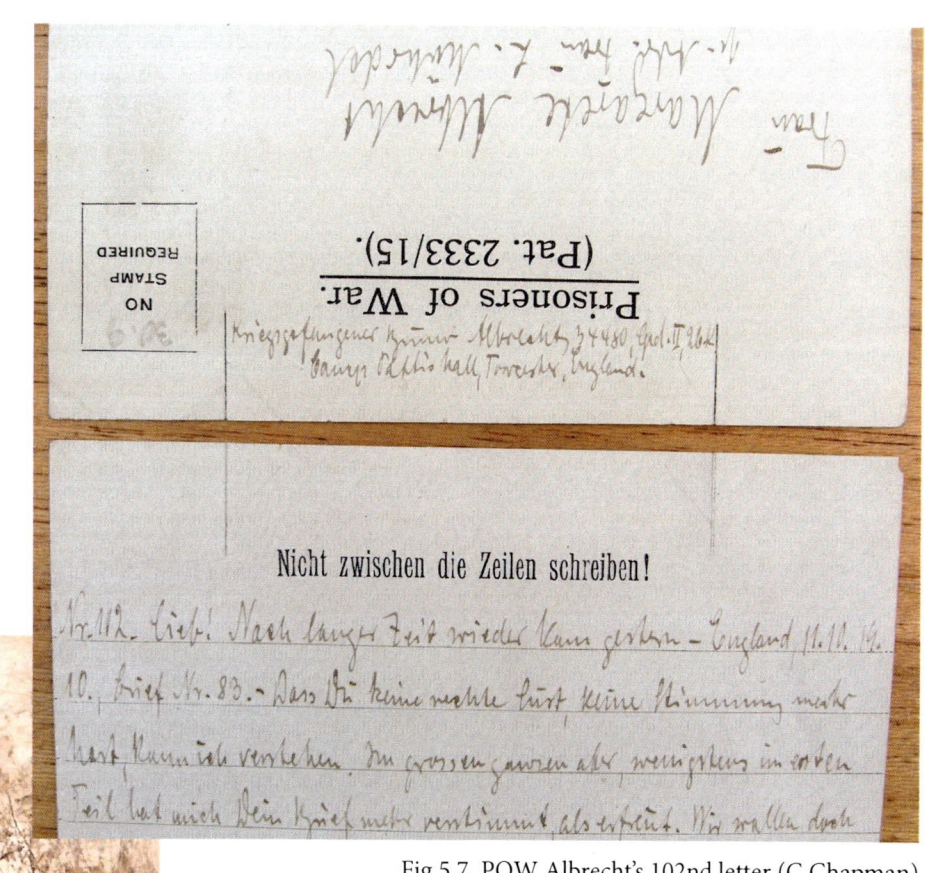

Fig 5.7. POW Albrecht's 102nd letter (C Chapman)

Fig 5.8. Musketier Krental wearing Iron Cross (W Palang)

Fig 5.9. The Orotava (W Palang)

Fig 5.10. POW Krental at Mendlesham (W Palang)

6. THE CAMP: Phase III
post-1919

Immediately after The Great War, indeed well after the Treaty of Versailles, Pattishall POW Camp remained the responsibility of the War Office whilst the land on which it stood remained the property of the trustees of the Sailors' Union, the NSFU. However, in March 1920, as we described in Chapter 3, the Disposal Board of the Ministry of Munitions inserted an advertisement in the *Northampton Mercury* and other papers for the sale of huts, building materials and Royal Engineers' stores. We have already detailed the considerable number of items offered in the sale, handled by Auctioneers Messrs Wise and Bowerman of Oxford and London. For those wishing to view the items in 1920 during the week prior to the sale, numbered catalogues could be obtained from the auctioneers or the Area Disposal Officer, Charing Cross Huts [*sic*], London. The Ministry indicated the accessibility of the Camp by rail and road from Northampton, Blisworth Junction Station and Towcester. The sale was scheduled for Tuesday, Wednesday, Thursday, 23rd, 24th, 25th March 1920 starting at 11am each morning.

We understand from local memory [Ref.6.1] that Pattishall Parish Council debated attendance at the sale. It is maintained that some councillors encouraged the Clerk to bid for the sewage disposal unit, but the notion was turned down on grounds of cost and the argument that what had suited their grandparents, often an earth-closet, suited them likewise. The parishioners had to wait until the 1950s for such a facility to be constructed.

Seemingly, even after the March sale there was still much from the Camp to be disposed of, for another sale was planned at Pattishall for 20th August 1920, again under the auspices of Wise and Bowerman. *The Times* of 18th August carried an advertisement, conspicuous in which were "two excellent brick and weather-boarded buildings 111ft x 61ft and 90ft x 54ft, with steel truss Belfast roofs, used as a theatre and QM Stores and very suitable for use as Village Halls, Chapels, Cinemas, or Concert Rooms". There were also five dining huts each 200ft by 30ft. At least two of the single-storey wooden buildings being offered for sale had been built outside of the Camp boundary in School Road for the benefit of the guards after the War Office took over in 1915 - both were bought by Henry James Hawtin. The former mess room, alongside the village school opposite the junction with Bird's Hill

Road, was subsequently used by the parish as a village hall (Fig.6.1) and became a familiar venue for many of the older parishioners. Card-parties, beetle-drives, Christmas and Old-Folks' parties, and meetings of uniformed organisations were all held there until 1977 when the new village hall was opened. The other wooden building became the home of a branch of the Howe family who lived there until it was later replaced by a brick-built house. It seems likely that also from this August sale, Abington Motors Ltd eventually acquired what became their garage and car showrooms in Wellingborough Road, Northampton, and Smith's Timber adapted another building for one of their warehouses near South Bridge, in Cotton End, Northampton.

Father Hopkins died on 24th March 1922, but in his will there is no mention of the land at Eastcote that he purchased in 1915 jointly with McGhee for the Camp; he refers only to his property at Alton Abbey, although he appoints a resident at Greenwich Priory as one of his executors. Wilson did not die until 16th April 1929 but neither Eastcote House nor the Camp feature in any memorials written on his demise. It appears that McGhee alone, Trustee of the NSFU, sold the estate on 23rd July 1923 to four Northamptonshire Stanford brothers. Later in the year, on 26th November, the Stanfords – Edwin a farmer in Pattishall, Walter, a cow-keeper in Nether Heyford, Alfred, a pianoforte tuner at 9, Marefair Northampton and Harry, a painter in Old Duston, as joint freehold tenants in common, sold Eastcote House to [retired] Captain Joseph Denby Ashley of Bournemouth for £1,287. 10s; with the house, Ashley acquired the stables, yard and gardens, woodland and paddock, but not the remainder of the estate on which much of the Camp had stood. The map accompanying the conveyance gave details of the water supply from the hydraulic ram to the house and cottages as well as sewerage facilities. With the agreement of Alfred Stanford and Joseph Frederick Davies who lived in an adjacent cottage, Ashley had access along the roadway from Bird's Hill Road to the former main access point into the Camp.

On 20th November 1925 the *Northampton Mercury* reported:
"Thirty-one German prisoners of war, who died in the internment camp at Eastcote during the Great War have had their last resting place in a corner of Pattishall burial ground permanently marked. From Germany there arrived, appropriately on Armistice Day, a consignment of memorial stones, which have been placed in position by a Towcester firm of monumental masons....arranged through..... the Imperial War Graves Commission."

The editor saw this as "…. a sign of the healing effect of time on the wounds the war left between the belligerent nations…." adding that "No one will grudge to the Germans….. that these few feet of English earth are theirs." (Fig.6.2) However, such apparent generosity of spirit was not so sincere, for he then went on to declare these few feet were "…all that they succeeded in retaining of the England against which they aimed their blow. A pathetic conquest!" Some seven years after the Armistice the *Mercury's* editor obviously had quite mixed feelings.

It was a sad irony for these young men captured in a terrible war only to die in the quiet seclusion of a Northamptonshire village in the flowering days of their manhood. In World War II there was no POW Camp at Eastcote, although evacuees from the Blitz were hosted in the village. One of these, Margaret Anne Barber, having been evacuated from Lowestoft to Rose Cottage, Pattishall, died aged 66 and was buried on 27th September 1940.

In September 1936 Edwin Stanford – previously living in Pattishall but then a farmer at Stone Pit Farm, Boughton - signed a Deed of Partition dividing the 'Camp' (as they called the fields on which the POWs were housed) amongst the brothers for their own use to sell or for rental. In the course of years this is precisely what happened. Walter Stanford remained at Heyford, Alfred retired to Grimscote and one of the brothers was the last resident of Mill House on the Banbury Lane before it was demolished. Much of the Camp site was leased to other farmers until bought from the Stanfords by Robert Hawtin in 1975.

Messrs Norman Moore, Don Hart, and Austin Nightingale, among others, subsequently purchased plots of former Camp land and built houses alongside the main access road from Bird's Hill Road to the Camp. Robert Hawtin turned the remainder of the Camp fields to grazing for sheep and cattle and he tells us that the holes and hollows left on the Camp grounds were gradually filled in over the years. It was in those fields that children from Pattishall Village School used to play.

Eastcote House remained in the ownership of Captain Ashley until 1943 when, in straitened circumstances, he was obliged to put it up for sale. Jackson, Stops and Staff, auctioneers in Northampton, advertised the sale in *Country Life* issued on 19th November 1943. The advertisement stressed the pretty garden, the Company's electric lighting, 9 bedrooms, 2 bathrooms, hall, 2 reception rooms, garage and stabling - all on 3 acres of land. In fact, the sale comprised the buildings and stables, and 3 acres and 22 perches of land, made up of the residence, stables, yard and garden occupying 1.155 acres, the paddock 1.355 acres, and woodland 0.626 acres. The property was bought on 7th November 1944 by Herbert Norman, an architect from Northampton who split off some rooms on the south side of the main house and named these Eastcote Lodge. When he died on 23rd July 1946 at the age of 78, both Eastcote House and Eastcote Lodge passed to his wife Phebe Norman but within four months she also died and their only daughter, Miss Mary Phebe Norman inherited Eastcote House and Lodge. Harry Ashton Hopper, a horse dealer and his wife Mary rented Eastcote Lodge and then on 30th Jan 1947 Miss M P Norman, who had remained in her Northampton home, leased the entire building to Donald Saunders Cockram for five years at £95 per annum. Cockram obviously enjoyed living there sufficiently, before his lease had expired, for him to purchase both Eastcote House and Lodge from Miss Norman for £3,150 on 26th July 1949; included in this sale were the stables, 3 acres 20 perches of land. Cockram stayed at the property for only seven months before selling it on 22nd February 1950 to Charles Henry Cocks for £2,500. Initially, Cocks lived in Eastcote House and his daughter, Patricia Jill Elkington, who had married George Elkington in the Summer of 1947, lived in Eastcote Lodge with her family.

When the Elkingtons moved to Everdon, Cocks sold Eastcote Lodge and the stables to Jack Jones who subsequently sold these to Ernest Reginald Bird. On 9th September 1957 Cocks granted Bird right of access to the paddock and the following day sold him part of the paddock and the right of access to it. Six months later, on 29th March 1958, Cocks sold Eastcote House to Frederick Hopkins for £2,500. Hopkins later sold the house to Leonard P Englert a shoe manufacturer of Northampton who, on 7th December 1973 sold it to Kenneth Charles Chick. Ernest Reginald Bird (known as Reg) and his wife Geraldine Mary (known as Dolly) remained living in Eastcote Lodge and owning the stables. Chick built a new home in part of the Eastcote House garden and on 28th May 1982 sold Eastcote House and the remaining land to Mrs Patricia Rowden where she and her husband now live as its present occupants. In 1988 the stables were converted into a dwelling house and it and Eastcote Lodge have remained as separate residences with successive different owners and occupiers over successive years.

On 16th October 1959 an agreement was reached between the governments of the United Kingdom and the Federal Republic of Germany which provided for the transfer to a central cemetery in the UK of all German casualties interred in British soil, except for those buried in Commonwealth cemeteries and plots maintained by the Commonwealth War Graves Commission. Accordingly, the Volksbund Deutsche Kriegsgräberfürsorge (German War Graves Commission) made arrangements for the dispersed remains of German combatants and civilians of both world wars to be moved to a new War Graves Cemetery at Cannock Chase in Staffordshire.

All those who had died while in Eastcote/Pattishall Camp were exhumed in the 1960s from the churchyard extension in Pattishall and reburied at Cannock (Fig.6.3). It may be pertinent to note here that from the cemetery at Alton Abbey, the NSFU's first internment camp for its German members (see Chapter 1), two merchant seamen, Edward Stelter (42) and Josef Wighard (21), were also disinterred and re-buried at Cannock Chase. That cemetery in Staffordshire, having a total of 2,143 casualties who died on British soil, was dedicated in June 1967. It is a moving and saddening sight to see so many lives lost for so many uncertain causes.

When one of the former buildings associated with the Camp, Pattishall Village Hall, was replaced in 1977, the former Guards' mess room with all its associations - the footfall of merchant seamen, military POWs, and the sound of children at play - disappeared into the parishioners' collective memory.

Fig 6.1. Camp Guards' Quarters, later Pattishall Village Hall (I Illingworth)

Fig 6.2. POW Graves in Pattishall Churchyard Extension (I Illingworth)

Fig 6.3. Pattishall POW Graves at Cannock Chase (C Chapman)

Dates of Deaths and Burials of POWs in Pattishall Church Yard Extension

Name	Date of Death	Age	Date of Burial	Total Camp Burials	Total Parish Burials
1915				1	9
Möller, Karl	5 Aug	64	5 Aug		
1916				1	15
Gumpert, Emil	28 Jan	47	1 Feb		
1917				5	13
Blum, Georg	16 Feb	40	21 Feb		
Pichotzke, Otto	20 Jun	33	16 Jun	[recorded date obviously in error]	
Knappe, Wilhelm	21 Jun	30	23 Jun		
Jost, Wilhelm	1 Jul	27	4 Jul		
Müller, Willy	13 Jul	21	16 Jul		
1918				11	22
Matthes, Ernst E	7 Aug	48	9 Aug		
Weissenborn, Richard	22 Oct	21	27 Oct		
Kiesow, Karl	7 Nov	21	12 Nov		
Esser, Friedrich	13 Nov	38	18 Nov		
Herold, Wilhelm	16 Nov	29	20 Nov		
Mezger, Georg	17 Nov	31	20 Nov		
Haake, Heinrich K A	18 Nov	30	21 Nov		
Becker, Diedrich	22 Nov	22	26 Nov		
Jacobi, Friedrich L	24 Nov	23	28 Nov		
Kunze, Hermann F	28 Nov	27	2 Dec		
Szymura, Anton	4 Dec	34	9 Dec		
1919				15	23
Marquardt, Robert	2 Feb	27	4 Feb		
Dunemann, Karl	9 Feb	28	13 Feb		
Meine, Amandus	4 Mar	33	10 Mar		
Günter, Johann	18 Mar	35	24 Mar		
Müller, Erich M	22 Mar	25	26 Mar		
Toepelt, August W	27 Mar	23	31 Mar		
Lesk, Otto	30 Mar	21	4 Apr		
Koperniak, Stanislaus	2 Apr	39	7 Apr		
Sandtner, Ludwig	28 Apr	23	2 May		
Fürnrohr, Andreas	15 May	35	14 May		
Heuer, Heinrich	7 Jul	22	10 Jul		
Koopmann, Christian	24 Aug	38	27 Aug		
Pellander, Max W	30 Aug	20	2 Sep		
Stielicke, August	30 Aug	39	4 Sep		
Kuhle, Fritz	10 Sep	31	*		

* Burial not in parish register but death recorded by civil registrar & grave identified when body exhumed in 1963.

EPILOGUE

The Camp at Eastcote overlaid fields of an earlier world. Robert Hawtin, farmer, knows their names:

'Home Ground' – where the Camp stood, 'Clapgate Close' – where Austin Nightingale built his house, 'Long Field' – where the osier beds stand and the reservoir was built, 'Elm Tree Close' [acquired by Father Hopkins and Richard McGhee] standing close to School Road, and the old ridge-and-furrow 'Linen Ground' – alongside Pound Lane and recalled as the Drying Ground possibly associated with the camp laundry.

In 1917, on 24th September, Pattishall School's Head Teacher recorded in her log book that she and her assistant had taken Classes I and II out to "get blackberries for the Army and Navy. The Babies' Class spent their half holiday at home as the Head thought the occupation too tiring for such little ones." At that time, with the POW camp standing opposite the school, the children would have looked further than Camp Field for their blackberries.

Two generations later, Marion Waller, former Deputy Head Teacher of Pattishall Primary School, wrote of the same Camp Field:
"That field…must be the school's richest free resource, which I used a lot…Nature walks with wild flower surveys through the seasons…the greatly loved 'Brook Walks' where we paddled… for a morning with buckets and yoghurt pots, collecting creatures and plants to take back to school to set up a big aquarium…that same field to which we all went across the road and sat among the buttercups whilst I read 'Alice Through The Looking Glass'."

Those men, whose letters we have read and whose inkpots once lay scattered in the earth, walked the same fields, made and sailed their model boats, dug their gardens and set their flower-beds, played football and waited so long for a terrible war to end. Their lives and hopes, cherished those many years ago, merit some form of honour which we hope this book will have provided. We all need to remember them before our world moves on and they are entirely forgotten. The men in the Camp and the children of Pattishall among the buttercups are depicted on our cover. It is to them all that this study is dedicated.

BIBLIOGRAPHY AND REFERENCES

Chapman, C R. *Pattishall, Enemy Aliens & 160 Dependent POW Camps, 1914-20.* In preparation.
Cohen-Portheim, P. *Time Stood Still: My Internment In England 1914-1918.* Kemp Hall Press. 1931.
Gallinger, A. *The Counter Charge: the Matter of War Criminals from the German Side.* Süddeutsche Monatshefte. 1922.
Mark, G. *Prisoners of War in British Hands during WWI.* Postal History Society. 2007.
Moss, R & Illingworth, I. *Pattishall, A Parish Patchwork.* Millcop. 2000.
The National Archives. ADM137, ADM186, CAB45, FO369, FO383, HO45, HO282, NATS1, RG9, RG10, RG11, RG14, WO162 and WO900 series.
Tupper, E. *Seamen's Torch.* Hutchinson. 1938.
University of Warwick, Modern Records Centre. NSFU Archive.
Wilson, H W and Hammerton, J A, eds. *The Great War.* Amalgamated Press. 1918.
Yarnall, J. *Barbed Wire Disease.* The History Press. 2011.
Deutsche Kriegsgefangene in Feindesland, Amtliches Material, England. Walter de Gruyter & Co. 1919.

Ref. 1.1. NSFU Finance Committee Minutes, Uni of Warwick. MSS.175/1/2/2.
Ref. 1.2. Northamptonshire Record Office (NRO). LG33/8, p.155.
Ref. 2.1. Tupper, E. *Op. Cit.* pp.112-13.
Ref. 3.1. Mary Evans Picture Library. Robert Hunt/ME 10272315.
Ref. 3.2. Pattishall School Log Book in NRO. P254/210, p.227. **Note**: Restricted Access.
Ref. 3.3. Mark, G. *Op .Cit.* p.212.
Ref. 3.4. Montgomery, Bob of Duston to Dr F Foden; letter 15 Dec 1992.
Ref. 3.5. Wilson, E M of Northampton to Dr F Foden; letter 19 Dec 1992.
Ref. 4.1. Gustav Lutz, on being re-captured in Suffolk in May 1917. *East Suffolk Gazette*, 8 May 1917, p.8, col.D.
Ref. 4.2. Mark, G. *Op. Cit.* pp.235-247.
Ref. 4.3. Machray, R; in Wilson, H W and Hammerton, J A. *Op.Cit.* Vol 12, p.401.
Ref. 4.4. *The Times*. 1 September 1917.
Ref. 5.1. Cohen-Portheim, P. *Op. Cit.* p.91.
Ref. 5.2. Gallinger, A. *Op. Cit.* pp. 102-3. (Cited in Yarnall, J. p.154.)
Ref. 5.3. Mark, G. *Op. Cit.* p.28.
Ref. 5.4. Mark, G. *Op. Cit.* p.157.
Ref. 5.5. *The Times*. 17 November 1999.
Ref. 6.1. Robert Hawtin et al; personal communications.

INDEX OF NAMES

Acland, R H D	27,34
Alber, D, POW No.3063	31
Albrecht, Bruno, POW No.4912, & POW No. 34480 & family	45
Adkins, Sir (William) Ryland	14
Ansley, Col. John Henry	19,20,27,38,39
Anstruther, Col Charles	27,34
Ashley, Captain Joseph Denby	53,54
August family	38
Ball, Max Frederick, POW	34
Barber, Margaret Anne	54
Bartmann, Andreas, POW No.18709	26
Beal, Boylston A	20,21
Becker, Diedrich, POW	57
Becker, Walter, POW No.32878	45
Belfield, Sir Herbert	7
Berwig, Fritz, POW No 16574	45,46,49
Berwig, Maria	45,46
Bird, Ernest Reginald (Reg)	55
Bird, Geraldine Mary (Dolly)	55
Blum, Georg, POW	50,57
Bohlert, POW (79 Inf. Regt.)	31
Böhm family	46
Böhm, POW No.3135	41
Bölle, Julius, POW No. 3123	44
Bond, Dr Charles J	9
Bone, Mrs	28
Bowerman, Charles	13
Brantingham, Francis E	21,22,23,24
Brauckhoff, Wilhelm, POW No. 247	21
Brunner, Arthur, POW No.1390	38
Burgh	35
Burr, Sir William	9
Bussacker, H, POW No.32925	31
Büttel, POW No.3142	41
Byrne, Sir William	7,16
Caplan, Max, POW No.26207	45
Chapman, Colin R	8,22,36,59
Chick, Kenneth Charles	55
Chilver, PC	35
Churchill, Winston	5
Clauberg, Ernst, POW No.2079	38
Cockram, Donald Saunders	55
Cocks, Charles Henry	55
Cohen-Portheim, Paul	37,59
Copeman, Regt Q'master-Sgt	51
Coy, John	36
Dalziel, Sir (James) Henry	14
Dauber, POW No.6580	41
Davies, Joseph Frederick	53
de Sturler, Dr A	30
de Sturler, R	30
Dresdner, W, POW No.10765	31
Duddeck, W	31
Dunemann, Karl, POW	57
Elkington, George & Jill	55
Englert, Leonard P	55
Esser, Friedrich, POW	57
Fawcett, Col Henry H	9
Foulger, Major F E	27,31
Frey, Carl & Head Teacher Frey	46
Friche, Karl	47
Fürnrohr, Andreas, POW	57
Gallinger, August	37,59
Gibson, Rev George	9,50
Gibson, Thomas	35
Gillitzer, Mari	26
Gitzen, Wilhelm, POW	34
Grattan, Col O'Donnell Colley	27,30
Gresham, Constance	1,2,4,6
Gresham, Frederick	1,2,4
Groom, George E	8
Grove, Philip	2
Gruhlen, Otto, POW	35
Gumpert, Emil, POW	50,57
Günter, Johann, POW	57
Haake, Heinrich, POW	57
Halcombe, Constance Ida	2
Hammerton, J A	59
Hart, Don	54
Harte, Herman, POW	34
Harvey, Sir Paul	7
Hawtin, Henry James	18,52
Hawtin, Robert	18,19,26,54,58,59
Herold, Wilhelm, POW	57
Heuer, Heinrich, POW	57
Höflings, Marie	26

Hopkins, Charles Plomer (Rev)	1,4,5,6, 11,12,17, 53,58	Mark, Graham	23,32, 36,59
Hopkins, Frederick	55	Markel, Dr K E	8,19,27,28
Hopper, Harry Ashton, & Mary	55	Marquardt, Robert, POW	57
Horner, Frederick, POW	36	Marshall, Howard	12,15,17
Hornsby, Florence	11	Martens, POW	30
Howe, Arthur	36	McGhee, Richard	1,4,5,6,11, 17,53,58
Howe family	53	McKenna, Reginald	13
Howes, Thomas & Mary Gleed	2	Meine, Amandus, POW	57
Illingworth, Iris	59	Mezger, Georg, POW	57
Jackson, Stops and Staff	54	Miller, Margaret	21
Jacobi, Friedrich, POW	57	Moll, Carl, POW	47
Jahn, Max	44	Möller, Karl, POW	50,57
Jameson, Sir Starr	8	Montgomery, Bob	59
Jaskutla, Theodore, POW	35	Moore, Norman	54
Jones, Jack	55	Moss, Richard	59
Jost, Wilhelm, POW	57	Mossinger, POW (Pion. Regt. 25)	31
Karle, Emil, POW No.18701	43	Muller, Heinrich, POW	34
Kerst, Arthur, POW	34	Müller, Erich, POW	57
Kesler, Leutnant D.R.	47	Müller, Joseph, POW No. 5376	44
Kiefer, Emil, POW No. 5370	43	Müller, Willy, POW	57
Kiesow, Karl, POW	57	Neuberger, Friedrich (Fritz), POW No.15155	44
Kingston, John William	11		
Kitchener, Lord Horatio Herbert	21	Nightingale, Austin	26,42, 54,58
Knappe, Wilhelm, POW	57		
Koopmann, Christian, POW	57	Nightingale, William	36
Koperniak, Stanislaus, POW	57	Nolte, POW (472 Inf. Regt.),	31
Kornith family	43	Norman, Herbert & Phebe	55
Kornith, Wilhelm, POW No. 15022	43	Norman, Mary Phebe	55
Krauplatz, Alf, POW No.12640	26	O'Brien, Pat(rick)	14
Krauplatz, Linette	26	Ogborn, Pte Ed, 44714	27
Krental, Albert, POW No.19935 & family	46,47, 48,50	Paland, Wolfgang	46,47
		Paland, Elizabeth	47
Kuhle, Fritz, POW	51,57	Pellander, Max, POW	50,57
Kunz, Hermann, POW	57	Phillipp, Councillor	43
Landes, Wilhelm, POW	33	Phipps, Matthew Wise & Sarah	2
Lees, Jonathan	25	Pichotzke, Otto, POW	57
Lesk, Otto, POW	50,57	Pirkins, Thomas & Sarah	1
Liddington, Ron	15	Redley, PC	35
Lieck, Albert	6	Reinhold, G, POW & family	26
Lloyd George, David	13,21	Rivera, Walter, POW	33
Lorenz, L, POW No.11743	31	Roberts, George Henry	14
Lowry, Edward G	8,18,19,20	Robertson, General William	21
Lutz, Lt, Gustav, POW	33,34,59	Rose, Capt.	30
MacCallum, J.D.Kellie	7	Rowden, Pat & David	55
Machray, Robert	32,59	Salbenblatt, Richard, POW	44
Malsbury, Albert	11	Sandtner, Ludwig, POW	51,57
		Schaper, POW (Ul. Regt. 11)	31

Scheffel, POW	30	Turner, Lieut Dr A J	27,30
Schinhofen, P, POW No.11538	31	Urbaučich, Maria	38
Schlesinger, POW	30	Vischer, Dr A L	30
Schmidt, Günter & family	42,43	von Reuter, Admiral Ludwig	49
Schmidt, Henrick, POW	35	von Schweinichen, Fähnrich, POW	23
Schmidt, Joseph, POW No. 23146	42	Wadewitz, Paul, POW No.21773	45
Schmiemann, POW No. 35513	31	Wal (surname unknown)	27
Schroeder, Herman, POW No.31131	48,49,50	Waller, Marion	58
		Watts, Frederick	51
Schulte, Wilhelm, POW	34	Weissenborn, Richard, POW	57
Schultz, Heinrich, POW	35	Wendel, 'big'	42
Schulz, Walter Herman, POW	34	Wetzel, Wilhelm, POW	33
Schwyzer, Dr Fritz	27,28,29	Wiedemann family	44
Seaman, PC	33	Wiedemann, Karl, POW No.18666	44
Shinwell, Emmanuel	5	Wiezel, Joseph, POW No.3999	43
Shortland, PC	35	Wighard, Josef, POW	56
Stanford brothers (A,E,H,& W)	53,54	Wilson, Joseph Havelock	1,4,5,6,8, 10,11,12 13,14,15, 16,17,26, 39,53
Starmer, Arthur	51		
Steinacher	42		
Stelter, Ewald, POW	56		
Stielicke, August, POW	57		
Stewart, Gershom	14	Wilson, E M	24,59
Stockhurst, Alfred, POW	32	Wilson, H W	59
Stöckl, Emil, POW No.3943	26	Wilson, William Tyson	14
Stops, William George	9,51	Wise and Bowerman	52
Strauss, Edward Anthony	14	Wiseman, James & Lydia	2,4
Szymura, Anton, POW	57	Wiseman, John Francis & Constance	1,2,4
Thamm, POW	30		
Toepelt, August, POW	51,57	Yarnall, John	59
Tompkins	35	Yoras, Hermann, POW	33
Tupper, Capt Edward	5,15,16,59	Zimmerlin, Forcart & Company	43

INDEX OF PLACES

Places below are located within the counties existing during the Great War. British Counties are identified in this index by code elements taken from the alpha-three Chapman County Code

Bdf = Bedfordshire, Bkm = Buckinghamshire, Brk = Berkshire, Cam = Cambridgeshire, Chs = Cheshire, Con = Cornwall, Dor = Dorset, Ess = Essex, Gla = Glamorgan, Ham = Hampshire, Hrt = Hertfordshire, IOM = Isle of Man, IOW = Isle of Wight, Ken = Kent, Ldn = London, Lei = Leicestershire, Nth = Northamptonshire, Rox = Roxburghshire, Rut = Rutland, Sal = Shropshire, Sfk = Suffolk, Sry = Surrey, Ssx = Sussex, Sts = Staffordshire, Yks = Yorkshire.

Note: Eastcote and Pattishall, and the nations/countries Britain and Germany, do not appear in this index, as they are mentioned frequently throughout the foregoing pages.

Abington, Cam	2
Aldershot, Sry	21
Alexandra Palace, North Ldn	18,20,25
Alton, Ham	4,5,6,10, 16,53,56
Austria	8,11,38
Barry Dock, Gla	4
Basel, Switzerland	43
Bavaria, Germany	26
Bechtshüttel, Germany	44
Bedfordshire	2
Beech, Ham	4
Belmont Hospital, Sry	48
Berlin, Germany	13,25,40, 43,45,47
Blackdown Camp, Sry	45
Blisworth, Nth	24,52
Boughton, Nth	54
Bournemouth, Dor	53
Brafield on the Green, Nth	35
Brocton, Sts	29
Burma	4
Buxton, Nfk	29
Calcutta, India	4
Cambridge, Cam	33
Cameroons, Africa	23
Cannock, Sts	56
Castlethorpe, Bkm	35
Clapham, South Ldn	27
Clapton, East Ldn	28
Cöpenick, Germany	45
Corby, Nth	22,29
Crewe, Chs	33
Crowthorne, Brk	28
Dalscote, Nth	16,24,42
Dalston German Hosp, East Ldn	20,21
Dartford, Ken	28
Denton, Nth	35
Donington Hall, Sal	25
Dorchester, Dor	23,25,39
Douglas, IOM	18,39,48
Dublin, Ireland	4
Eastcote, Mdx	26
Emberton, Bkm	2
Everdon, Nth	55
Falmouth, Con	44
Foster's Booth, Nth	15,19,32
France	30,37,44,47
Frith Hill, Sry	10,21,22,45
Geneva, Switzerland	8,13,18
Glasgow, Scotland	5
Glendon, Nth	29
Greenwich Priory, South Ldn	4,6
Grimscote, Nth	54
Hackleton, Nth	35
Halesworth, Sfk	33
Hamburg, Germany	45
Handforth, Chs	25,29,33
Hannover. Germany	44
Holland	3,30
Horsham, Ssx	4
Huntingdon, Hun	29

India	3,4	Peterborough, Nth	35
Ipswich, Sfk	33	Portsmouth, Ham	13
Ireland	5	Preston Deanery, Nth	35
Isle of Man	10,13,17, 18,49	Putney, South Ldn	2
		Rangoon, Burma	4
Isle of Wight	22	Reuss ältere Linie, Germany	44
Joyce Green, Ken	29	Ribecourt, France	44
Kegworth, Lei	32,34	Richborough, Ken	29
Kempten, Germany	45,46	Rothersthorpe, Nth	35
Kentish Town, North Ldn	11	Rothwell, Nth	35,43
Kidbrook, Ken	29	Roxburghshire	22
Kimbolton, Hun	27	Rutland	22,29
Knockaloe, IOM	17,18,22,37	Ryde, IOW	13
Lancaster, Lan	19	Salzgitter, Germany	46,47
Leigh, Lan	39	Sand's Farm, Nth	19
Lewes, Ssx	29	Scapa Flow, Scotland	49
Lincolnshire	22	Solingen, Germany	38
Linden, Germany	44	Somme, France	22,47
Linton, Cam	29	Sompting, Ssx	29
Liverpool, Chs	38	Southend, Ess	13
Lofthouse Park, Yrk	25,37	Southill, Bdf	29,35
London	4,10,13,17, 38,40,52	Southwold, Sfk	33
		St. Helena, South Atlantic	3
Loos, France	47	Stepney, East Ldn	6
Lowestoft, Sfk	54	Stobs, Rox	22,23
Madras, India	3	Stony Stratford, Bkm	35
Maldon, Ess	44	Suffolk	47
Marne, France	47	Surrey	10,21
Martlesham, Sfk	29	Sweden	3
Meiningen, Germany	26	Switzerland	3,30,43
Mendlesham, Sfk	48	Towcester, Nth	8,9,24,32, 40,51,52,53
Middlesborough, Yrk	5		
Narborough, Nfk	29	Transvaal, Eastern, Africa	3
Nether Heyford, Nth	53,54	Trieste, [Austria-Hungary*]	38
Neuville-Vitasse, Germany	47	United States of America	3
Nilgiri Hills, India	3	Uppingham, Rut	29
Northampton	2,10,12, 24,33,35, 52,53,55	Wash, The	22
		Washington DC, USA	31
		Watling Street [A5]	1
Nürnberg, Germany	26	Weedon, Nth	1,16
Old Duston, Nth	53	Whiston, Nth	35
Olympia, W Ldn	4	Wilhelmshaven, Germany	47
Orfordness, Sfk	48	Woburn, Bdf	22,29
Oswestry, Sal	39	Woking, Sry	23
Oxford	52	Wolverton, Bkm	35
Panshanger, Hrt	23,29	Wrentham, Sfk	33
Paris, France	49	York, Yks	4
Peel, IOM	18	Ypres, Belgium	46,47

*Trieste was formally annexed to Italy in 1920